MW00785858

A GUIDE TO
NEW YORK STATE
GOVERNMENT

ABOUT THE
LEAGUE OF WOMEN VOTERS

The League of Women Voters is a nonpartisan, volunteer, grassroots organization with a dual purpose—education and advocacy. The League was formed when women received the right to vote, and its initial purpose was to educate and empower these new voters. Today the League is still dedicated to keeping our democracy strong by giving women and men a voice in government.

Throughout its history, the League has considered voter education one of its most important functions. The League provides nonpartisan information on candidates and ballot issues, sponsors candidate forums, promotes voter registration, and encourages participation in the political process.

From its beginnings, the League has also been an advocacy organization. Today the League represents 100,000 women and men nationwide on a variety of issues. In New York State, the League supports the right to privacy in reproductive choice, uniform access and eligibility for health care, improved ballot access and public financing for election campaigns, merit selection of judges and merger of the major trial courts, alternatives to incarceration for nonviolent offenders, a ban on assault weapons, protection of our environment, and open and responsive government.

The Foundation for Citizen Education is the educational affiliate of the League of Women Voters of New York State. The Foundation operates a toll-free telephone hotline providing information on local, state, and federal issues and operations; publishes pamphlets and books about voting and government; promotes citizen education in schools; and supports the educational projects of local Leagues throughout the state.

A GUIDE TO
NEW YORK STATE
GOVERNMENT

Seventh Edition

Foundation for Citizen Education
of the
**LEAGUE OF WOMEN VOTERS
OF NEW YORK STATE**

Mary Jo Fairbanks, Editor

POLICY STUDIES ASSOCIATES
P.O. Box 337
Croton-on-Hudson, New York 10520

Published and distributed for the League of Women Voters of New York State
by Policy Studies Associates (PSA), Box 337, Croton-on-Hudson, NY 10520.
PSA is a division of the Council on International and Public Affairs, 777 United
Nations Plaza, New York, NY 10017.

Library of Congress Cataloging-in-Publication Data

A guide to New York State government / the League of Women Voters of
    New York State ; Mary Jo Fairbanks, editor. — 7th ed.
        p.   cm.
    Includes bibliographical references and index.
    ISBN 0-936826-41-X
    1. New York (State)—Politics and government—Handbooks, manuals, etc.
    I. Fairbanks, Mary Jo, 1939-   . II. League of Women Voters of New York
    State.
    JK3431. G85 1995
    320. 4747—dc20
                                                            94-29505
                                                            CIP

Cover Design by Warren Hurley
Typesetting and formatting by Peggy Hurley

Manufactured in the United States of America

CONTENTS

PART ONE: NEW YORK STATE GOVERNMENT

PART TWO: LOCAL GOVERNMENT

LIST OF FIGURES AND TABLES

PREFACE AND ACKNOWLEDGMENTS

This *Guide to New York State Government* first appeared 40 years ago under the title *New York State: A Citizen's Handbook*. The League's goal was to prepare an overview of state government that would be comprehensive and understandable. This latest edition, the seventh, follows in that tradition. Although written primarily for use by high school students, it is an excellent resource for all New York residents interested in the workings of their state government.

Since its founding 75 years ago, the League has encouraged citizen participation in government. The key to participation is information. Understanding the responsibilities and functions of the various branches of state government enables citizens to become effective advocates for issues they consider important and to evaluate the performance of their representatives.

Originally a slim volume, this new edition reflects the growth in state government over the past 40 years. The New York State Legislature has taken on greater and more complex responsibilities in response to a more complex society demanding greater government services. The state university system has developed and expanded, environment-related agencies have burgeoned, and the judicial system has changed. Once the meeting place of a part-time legislature, Albany has become the center of year-round state government.

The League gratefully acknowledges that this present edition rests on the contributions in time and talents of all the writers, experts, and consultants to the previous editions. This edition was produced under the direction of Barbara Johnsen, Communications Vice President, and Anne Nelson, Publications Chair. Members of the present and past state League board updated or rewrote the entire volume. Their names and the names of the specialists outside of the League who contributed their expertise are found at the beginning of each chapter. Final editing was done by Mary Jo Fairbanks, editor of the sixth edition. Paul Wm. Bradley, formerly on the League staff and a catalytic force for the last edition, served as a reader.

We are again pleased to be associated with Policy Studies Associates, who, as our publisher, helps us to reach a far wider market with this book. Special thanks also to the PSA production editor, Cynthia Morehouse, and also a League member.

We hope *A Guide to New York State Government* will become a resource for all New York citizens and inspire them to become involved in the democratic process. This is the mission of the League of Women Voters; this is the essence of our democracy.

Evelyn M. Stock,
First Vice President, League of Women
Voters of New York State

PART ONE

NEW YORK STATE GOVERNMENT

1.
INTRODUCTION TO NEW YORK STATE*

RECENT HISTORY AND TRENDS

The outstanding quality of New York State is its vitality—its diverse people, industries, culture, and topography. Its richness and strength lie in its changing population, incorporating the established and the immigrant into a multicultural, multi-language population of 18 million people.

The only contacts that many New Yorkers have with state government are their driver's licenses and their income tax forms. State government, however, is involved in our lives in a myriad of other ways—education, environmental protection, prisons, gun control, welfare, and health care. Some problems now facing the state were almost unknown 20 years ago—homelessness and AIDS, for example.

For two expansive decades before 1975, New York lived by its motto—Excelsior! The state's policies and programs during the period gave it the nation's premier system of higher education and a well-deserved record of support for public schools, social services, and health care.

However, as Governor Hugh Carey said in his first State of the State message that year, everyone in the state had come to think of the state budget "as a cornucopia, a never-ending horn of plenty that

*By Shirley Eberly, President of the League of Women Voters of New York State, with acknowledgment to *Empire State Report* (April 1994).

3

could pay for more and more each year. . . . Now the time of plenty, the days of wine and roses, are over." The era of ever-expanding programs and taxes was coming to an end.

Only a month after Carey was sworn in, New York was hit by a major fiscal crisis, and the state's financial problems have, to a lesser degree, continued over the 20-year period since then. Over the past two decades, the size of the state budget has more than tripled, and the growing costs of social programs and meeting federal mandates are outstripping the growth of state revenues.

Inequities between urban and suburban schools have continued. The state's school aid formula continues to penalize poor communities and poor student populations. Although public school enrollment in New York over the past 20 years has declined by almost a million students, state budget allocations for school aid, fueled by the greater array of social services needed, have more than tripled.

In the early 1970s, Governor Nelson Rockefeller introduced a package of tough drug laws. At the same time, another piece of legislation, the second felony offender law, which dictates mandatory jail sentences regardless of circumstances, also went into effect. These two laws—plus the growing problems caused by drug addiction—have led to an explosive growth in the state's prison population, which has almost quintupled over the last 20 years, going from 12,000 to almost 60,000, with arrests for drug offenses growing from 38,000 to 90,000.

Environmental problems have been with us at least since the early 1980s, although the state's total waste generation has leveled off from previous years. Local governments, which must deal with 6.1 pounds of waste per resident per day, have struggled to move from landfills to incineration and recycling. Passage of the "bottle bill" in 1982, however, has reduced the need for landfill space and has resulted in cleaner roadsides. Two major environmental issues still must be dealt with—the problem of air pollution and that of locating storage sites for nuclear waste. Most of New York's air pollution is generated by cars and other vehicles, which consume 40 percent of all energy used in the state. The state's low-level radioactive waste storage facility in West Valley was closed in 1975, yet the state has still not solved the problem of where to locate permanent storage sites for both low-level and solid nuclear waste.

Our state has immense strengths to seek innovative, cooperative solutions to the challenges that we face now and that lie ahead in the twenty-first century. Each year, in attempts to deal with these problems, about 15,000 bills are introduced into the state legislature—and lobbyists now spend almost $35 million trying to influence the outcome. Therefore, it is vital that citizens pay close attention to what happens in Albany and that they continue to let their legislators know their views on important public issues.

THE STATE CONSTITUTION

The basic law by which a democratic nation or state is governed is its constitution, which sets forth provisions establishing governmental goals, organizational structure, and limitations. We Americans are a constitution-making people, and the writing of our basic law has become symbolic of our self-government.

The constitution of the State of New York is subordinate only to the federal constitution and statutes. Founded on the doctrine that the authority of government is derived from the people, it specifies that every provision must be approved by popular vote. Some sections have remained unchanged since their adoption in 1777, while others embody needs and convictions of succeeding generations.

State constitutions are generally much longer and more detailed than the United States Constitution, which is brief, broad, and general. The more flexible nature of the federal constitution allows for redefinition and reinterpretation without amendment. Most state constitutions, on the other hand, require frequent amendment to eliminate obsolete sections and to adjust the limits of state and local powers to contemporary needs.

The New York State Constitution creates our structure of government, which consists of a governor, a two-house legislature, a state-wide court system, and a system of local governments. It defines the powers of and limitations on our elected officials, as well as the matters which may be decided through legislation and those which the voters decide. It protects our civil rights, such as the right to trial by jury, freedom of speech, and the right to bargain collectively.

The New York State Constitution may be amended in two ways—either by the legislative process or by a constitutional convention. Under the first method, an amendment may be proposed in either house of the legislature. It must be passed by two successive, separately elected legislatures and submitted to the people. If it is approved by a majority of those voting on the question, it becomes a part of the constitution. In the past, the ballot has contained in a single year as many as 11 such proposals, often of a highly controversial nature.

The constitution also provides that every 20 years the question, "Shall there be a convention to revise the Constitution and amend the same?" be placed on the ballot. The legislature may also place this question on the ballot at any other time that it wishes to do so. In 1977 state voters gave a resounding "no" when asked that question. It will appear again on the ballot in 1997 and, if a majority of voters decide that a convention is desirable, delegates will be elected in 1998 for a convention to be held in the spring of 1999. Convention delegates may revise the existing constitution or write a completely new one, but any change must be approved by voters.

At the time of independence, the constitution of the colony of New York was not a written document. Colonial government was based on Dutch and English customs and laws. In May 1776, the Continental Congress advised each colony to form a government of its own and to write a constitution. New York's Fourth Provisional Congress was elected specifically for this purpose. Constantly in danger of capture by the British, the delegates met in White Plains and later in Kingston. On April 20, 1777, the constitution they framed was adopted. While it embodied a profound belief in the inalienable rights of the individual, virtually all power in the state government was reserved to the landowners.

Nine conventions to revise the constitution have been held since. The convention of 1821 wrote the Bill of Rights into the basic state law. The era of Jacksonian democracy produced the constitution of 1846, reflecting expanding concepts of popular rights and government. The powers of the legislative and executive branches were curtailed, property qualifications for voting were removed, and most public offices were changed from appointive to elective.

When the 1894 convention met, corruption in government and bossism were the burning issues of the day. Distrust of public officials was coupled with the belief that the government had no part to play in the economic and social life of the times. This resulted in a constitution that, on one hand, placed severe restrictions on the legislature and, on the other, spelled out in minute detail policies intended to promote civic virtue. Among new provisions added were the merit system for civil service; limitations on the power to dispose of the state's forest preserves; and a strong state commitment to public education, public welfare, and the public health. This 1894 document, since amended more than 200 times, is our present constitution.

Three constitutional conventions have been held since 1894. The 1915 convention proposed 33 changes that were rejected by the voters, but many of these, such as the executive budget process, were later added by individual amendment. The convention of 1938 was unsuccessful in achieving its announced goal of simplifying the unduly complex document. Nevertheless, it did propose new concepts of public responsibility for social welfare, including public housing and unemployment insurance, which were approved, as was the right to unionize.

The latest attempt to streamline this archaic document took place in 1967, when the ninth constitutional convention assembled in Albany. Its announced purpose was threefold: to eliminate obsolete and confusing provisions and remove unnecessary detail (such as specifications of prizes that are permitted in bingo games); to reexamine constitutional provisions requiring referenda on state bond issues and barring joint government-private undertakings; and to establish methods of legislative districting that would meet the federal one-person/one-vote standard. Partisan politics controlled the convention proceedings, with the Assembly speaker acting as the convention's president. The proposed new document, submitted to the voters as a single package, went down to defeat at the polls, largely because of its proposed repeal of the "Blaine Amendment," a section of the constitution prohibiting state aid to church-related schools.

Today, many of the major issues facing New Yorkers are clearly constitutional in nature—basic rights, the scope of government power, and its taxing authority. Other issues, which people sometimes don't think of as being constitutional ones, concern education, our criminal justice system, low-income housing, and the state's canal system and forest preserves. In fact, most issues that New Yorkers say are important to them are embodied in the constitution.

Those who favor a constitutional convention believe that a complete overhaul is necessary in order to fundamentally change the way our state government works—or doesn't work. They believe that only a convention will be able to deal with such problems as legislative gridlock, expensive and unfunded state mandates on local governments, and irresponsible state borrowing and taxing procedures. However, others believe that a constitutional convention would endanger those rights that are now ensured by our constitution and would open a "Pandora's box" with the potential to undo much of what is good about New York State's government.

New York's constitution continues to be an untidy document, filled with minutiae and containing approximately 80,000 words (compared to Vermont's constitution containing 6,600 words). It is filled with lengthy exceptions to such sections as the state's forever wild provisions (such as those specifying the number and width of Adirondack ski trails and authorizing exchanges of small parcels of land for lengthening a local airport runway or establishing a landfill) and those forbidding gambling or wagering (but permitting bingo if the prize is not more than $250). Another kind of obsolescence comes not from amendments but from a continuation in the constitution of provisions which conflict with federal law, such as the suffrage article which still lists a minimum age of 21 and the ability to read and write English as qualifications for voting.

Some state governmental objectives can be accomplished through legislation, others only through constitutional revision. Excessive detail in a constitution results in inflexibility, which provides protection for basic rights and processes, insulating them from capricious action by the state legislature. However, such inflexibility also sometimes makes it difficult for our state government to function efficiently and effectively—and it creates often unnecessary barriers to change based on new circumstances and new challenges.

The state constitution consists of the following articles:

Article I: Bill of Rights
Article II: Suffrage
Article III: Legislature
Article IV: Executive
Article V: Officers and Civil Departments
Article VI: Judiciary
Article VII: State Finances
Article VIII: Local Finances
Article IX: Local Governments
Article X: Corporations
Article XI: Education
Article XII: Defense
Article XIII: Public Officers
Article XIV: Conservation
Article XV: Canals
Article XVI: Taxation
Article XVII: Social Welfare
Article XVIII: Housing
Article: XIX: Amendments to Constitution
Article XX: When to Take Effect

2.
THE EXECUTIVE BRANCH*

The executive branch of the government of New York State is headed by four officials who are elected by all voters of the state. In addition to the governor, these are the lieutenant-governor, the attorney-general, and the comptroller. All are elected to four-year terms in even-numbered, nonpresidential election years. These officials manage the many administrative departments and agencies that conduct the business of the government. Their annual salaries are set by the New York State Legislature and may be changed only by legislative action.

THE GOVERNOR

The governor of the state of New York is the single most important official of state government. As head of the state, the governor is constitutionally charged with implementing the laws of the state, and as chief administrator, oversees all state functions. Beyond administrative powers, the governor is endowed with executive, legislative, and political powers.

In addition to an annual salary, the governor is entitled to the use of the executive mansion in Albany as a residence. There is no restriction on the number of terms the governor may serve.

To qualify for the office of governor, a person must be a citizen of the United States, be at least 30 years old, and a resident of New York

*By Deborah Wenig.

State for at least five years prior to election.

A governor may be impeached by a majority vote of the Assembly. The impeachment must then be tried by a court consisting of the Senate and the judges of the Court of Appeals with a two-thirds majority of this court required for conviction. In the history of New York State, only one governor, William Sulzer, has been impeached and removed from office (in 1912).

Executive and Administrative Powers

The governor, as the state's chief administrator, oversees the management of all state departments and agencies. With the advice and consent of the Senate, the governor appoints the heads of most departments, boards, and commissions and may also remove them from office.

Three major department heads are not appointed by the governor. The attorney-general, who heads the Department of Law, and the comptroller, who heads the Department of Audit and Control, are both elected by the people. The commissioner of the Department of Education is appointed by the Board of Regents of the University of the State of New York.

Even with these exceptions to the governor's appointive powers, the right to examine and investigate the management and affairs of any department, board, agency, or commission contributes greatly to the control of state administration.

The governor's role in budget-making is another key factor in shaping the administration since the state's budget, prepared by the Division of the Budget (the head of which is appointed by the governor without Senate confirmation), reflects the policies and programs of the governor. Additionally, the expenditure plans of all departments must be approved by the governor.

To some extent, the governor also plays a role in the judicial branch of the government by appointing judges of the Court of Appeals and the Court of Claims with the advice and consent of the Senate. The governor also designates who will serve in the four Appellate Divisions of the court and fills vacancies on the Supreme Court, Surrogate's Court, County Court, Family Court (outside New York City), and District Court.

In cases of unusual or highly sensitive crimes, when it is considered that the local prosecutor's efforts will be hampered in providing a fair trial or when residents of a community are convinced that the prosecution will be biased, the governor may appoint a special prosecutor to handle the case.

The power of pardon is another quasi-judicial function of the governor. Except in cases of treason and impeachment, the governor may grant reprieves, commutations, and pardons after conviction. Even in cases of treason, the governor may suspend execution of sentence until the next meeting of the legislature, at which time the legislature assumes jurisdiction.

The governor also is empowered to appoint special commissions of investigation—known as Moreland Act Commissions—to inquire into the conduct in office of any public officer or body, as well as to examine any matter concerned with the execution or enforcement of state laws or the promotion of public peace, safety, and justice.

DID YOU KNOW . . . that the governor may remove certain locally elected officials, including district attorneys and sheriffs, for misconduct in office?

As Commander-in Chief of the New York State National Guard, the governor appoints its head and, with the consent of the Senate, all major-generals, each of whom must be federally qualified. The governor, using discretionary powers, assigns units of the guard to deal with emergencies that arise in any part of the state.

To a large degree, the governor's administrative functions are carried out by staff members in the executive department. Some of the important members of the governor's staff are the secretary, counsel, budget director, and communications director.

Legislative Powers

The governor is often called the state's chief legislator because many programs and policies originating in the governor's office heavily influence the agenda of each legislative session. The governor may not introduce bills to the legislature, although the governor's legislative program in the form of a large number of administration bills may be introduced by individual legislators. Usually the bills are introduced through legislative leaders or through heads of the committees concerned with the particular legislation. In this way, the governor's measures are assured a hearing.

The governor is required to report to the legislature at the beginning of each session in a "State of the State" message which outlines the state government's past accomplishments and the governor's future goals.

Among the governor's legislative powers is the requirement that an executive budget and supporting revenue proposals be submitted to the legislature. Until this century, New York State had a legislative budget system, but in 1927 a constitutional amendment established our current executive budget system. Governor Franklin Delano Roosevelt presented the first executive budget in 1929.

The power to veto bills of the New York State Legislature is another of the governor's legislative powers. In the 1821 constitution, the governor was granted package veto power for all legislation and item veto authority for appropriations bills. Although the executive budget system has decreased the need for the item veto, veto may be used by the governor for a number of reasons that include:

- poor drafting, technical errors
- premature, more study needed
- insufficient implementation time
- governor makes recommendation for changes

Limitations on the Governor's Powers

Although the governor's authority is extensive, it does have limitations. The governor can spend public money only when authorized by the legislature. A veto of legislation may be overridden by a two-thirds vote in each house of the legislature. The governor shares a measure of responsibility with the comptroller and attorney-general, but has little authority or control over them. Although the governor has the right to propose programs, they cannot be enacted without legislative approval. Finally, the need to obtain the consent of the Senate on many appointments, and the existence of boards with members who may have been appointed by a previous governor, substantially limit the governor's powers of appointment as well as control of policy-making boards.

Political Role of the Governor

The governor's influence is extended through the role as titular leader of a political party. From the time of nomination as a candidate, the governor, whose policy positions are normally reflected in the party's platform, acquires great political prestige. After election, high political standing helps the governor to shape legislation intended to carry out the party platform. The governor is naturally better able to see policies and programs adopted if the party also succeeds in electing a majority of the members of the legislature. The governor's ability to command public attention helps mobilize public opinion and focus it on legislative objectives.

Overall, the governor's effectiveness is enhanced by a research staff, by the information available through the administrative departments, by the part-time nature of the legislature as compared to the governor's full-time position, by the role of party leader, and by the high visibility of the office.

THE LIEUTENANT-GOVERNOR

Across the country as well as here in New York State, the lieutenant-governor's position has long been the brunt of jokes. The original lieutenant-governor joke is believed to have originated with Calvin Coolidge when he was serving as lieutenant-governor in Massachusetts.

The story goes . . . that at an official dinner Coolidge was asked by a woman what he did. He replied, "I'm the lieutenant-governor." That's wonderful," she said. "Tell me about it." "I just did," he replied.

Aside from what is constitutionally mandated, the governor and lieutenant-governor in consultation determine the additional roles the lieutenant-governor will carry out. Hence, the lieutenant-governor could be a partner in the administration of the executive branch or could simply be "standby equipment," as some political humorists allege.

The lieutenant-governor is elected on a joint ballot with the governor to insure that both will be of the same party. The constitution envisions the office of lieutenant-governor as a standby office to assure orderly succession should the governor be unable to serve for any reason—the so-called "heartbeat power." Should the lieutenant-governor, for any reason, succeed to the office of governor, no election would be held to fill the office of lieutenant-governor for the balance of the term. Proposals have been made to allow the governor power to appoint someone to the office of lieutenant-governor should it become vacant for any reason.

Duties of the Lieutenant-Governor

The constitution provides that the lieutenant-governor succeeds the governor when he is unable to serve. This includes stepping in for the governor whenever the governor leaves the state. According to the New York State Constitution Article IV:6, the lieutenant-governor is the president of the Senate but shall only cast a vote in case of a tie. These provisions enable involvement in the legislative process.

THE ATTORNEY-GENERAL

As head of the Department of Law, the attorney-general is the state's chief legal officer and provides legal services to departments and agencies of state government. In addition to civil responsibilities in these areas, the attorney-general prosecutes criminal violations of the labor, workers' compensation, unemployment, insurance, conservation, and tax laws.

Additionally, the attorney-general also prosecutes fraudulent sales of stocks and securities and violations of the General Business Law and is perhaps most widely known to the public for his ability to prosecute frauds against consumers.

The statewide Organized Crime Task Force is based in the attorney-general's office. Its function is to investigate and prosecute organized crime activities that cross county lines and to assist or, if necessary, supplant county district attorneys in that effort.

As the state's chief attorney, the attorney-general frequently serves as an advisor when there are questions about the constitutionality of bills and legislative acts.

THE COMPTROLLER

The comptroller is the chief fiscal officer of the state and heads the Department of Audit and Control, directing all of its activities related to cash management, state debt, and investment. This department audits the accounts and records of all state agencies and supervises the financial recordkeeping of more than 9,000 local governments, school districts, and other quasi-governmental bodies. The comptroller also administers the state retirement systems and the New York State Social Security Agency and is custodian of their funds.

VACANCIES

In case of vacancy in the offices of both governor and lieutenant-governor, or if both are impeached, absent from the state, or otherwise unable to serve, the Temporary President of the Senate serves as governor until the inabilities have ceased or until a governor is elected.

While acting as governor, if the Temporary President of the Senate is away from the state or is unable to serve for any reason (or if that office becomes vacant), the Speaker of the Assembly acts as governor.

3.
THE JUDICIAL BRANCH*

New York State has one of the most intricate court systems in the nation. It is divided geographically into four Judicial Departments, each with its own intermediate appeals court, known as the Appellate Division of the Supreme Court. Each Judicial Department is divided into Judicial Districts composed of one or more counties. A Supreme Court is located in each Judicial District. Altogether, the state has 12 Judicial Districts; half of these are located in the most heavily populated part of the state, the New York City metropolitan area (see Figure 3-1).

All courts in New York, except the federal courts, are part of the state's unified court system (see Figure 3-2). Although the state constitution defines in general terms the powers and duties of each court, it also gives the New York State Legislature limited power to determine the kinds of matters a particular court may consider. In addition, the constitution gives the legislature the power to establish and discontinue some lower courts. The constitution also sets judicial qualifications and provides for the selection and removal of judges.

To illustrate the complexity of the New York State court system, former Chief Judge of the Court of Appeals, Sol Wachtler, once had this to say:

*By Sydelle Herzberg, with special acknowledgment for court charts and overall review to Ivy Miller of the State of New York, Unified Court System, Office of Management Support, Office of Court Administration.

If I were to ask any one of you to describe the jurisdiction of the courts within our system, you could not do it. There are the Civil and Criminal Courts [see following page 39 for differences] in New York City which don't exist in Nassau County, where you have the District Court. But when you go across the City line you will find the jurisdiction of that Court has been absorbed by the Supreme Court. Appeals from our District Court go to the Appellate Term—not to be confused with the Appellate Division which is merely a division of the Supreme Court. And the Appellate Division and the Appellate Term should not be confused with the Court of Appeals which is the highest court in the state. The Court of Appeals is the supreme court but is not called the Supreme Court in this state. That title is reserved for the court which has unlimited original jurisdiction, that is, except when dealing with matters that must be resolved by the Surrogate's Court or the Family Court.
                    —Excerpt from a speech given in Nassau County

COURT STRUCTURE AND JURISDICTION

There are two fundamental types of courts: appellate courts that hear appeals from the decisions of other courts; and trial courts, also called courts of original jurisdiction, where cases begin. There are 11 different trial courts within the state system (see Figure 3-3).

Appellate Courts

THE COURT OF APPEALS

The Court of Appeals is the highest court in the state and is located in Albany. In state government, it is the equivalent of the United States Supreme Court. Generally, this court reviews questions of law. Individuals or groups may appeal directly from a trial court to the Court of Appeals if the question involved is restricted to constitutionality of either a state or federal statute.

The remainder of the calendar is controlled by the court and consists of hearing selected appeals from the Appellate Division. The court's decisions are final and can only be appealed to the United States Supreme Court in cases involving federal constitutional questions. The Court of Appeals is also responsible for determining policy

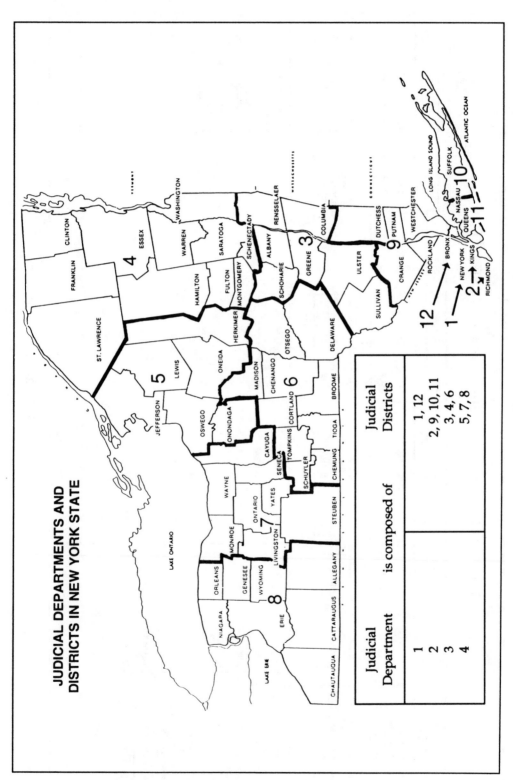

Figure 3-1

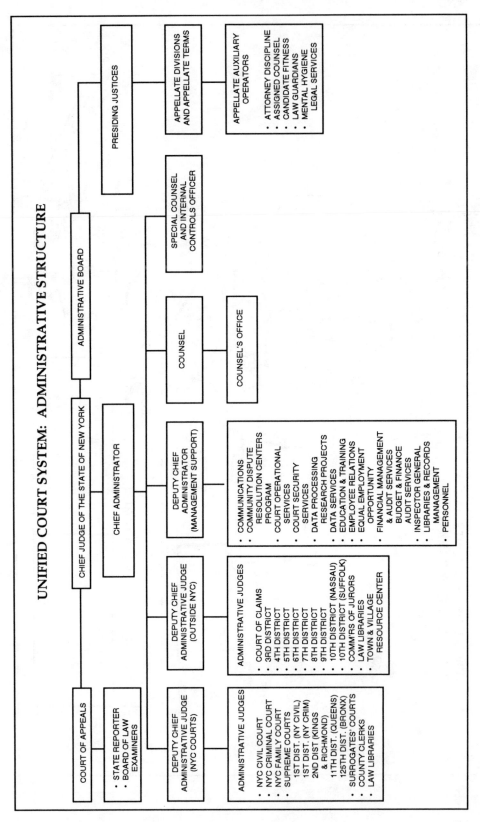

Figure 3-2

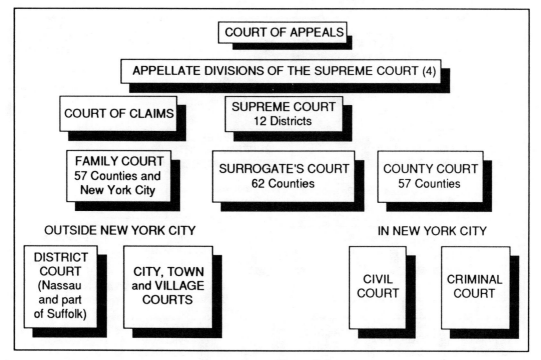

Figure 3-3: The Judiciary

for the administration of the entire court system in New York State.

The Court of Appeals consists of the Chief Judge and six Associate Judges. Five members of the court constitute a quorum, and concurrence (agreement) by four members is required for a decision.

THE APPELLATE DIVISIONS

The Appellate Division in each Judicial Department is the first level of appeals from five trial courts: Supreme, Family, Surrogate's, Court of Claims, and County Court. The responsibilities of the Appellate Divisions include resolving appeals from the trial courts in civil and criminal cases and conducting proceedings to admit, suspend, or disbar lawyers. Up to five justices may hear each case, but three must agree for a decision. Four justices constitute a quorum.

APPELLATE TERMS OF THE SUPREME COURT

The Appellate Division in each department may establish an Ap-

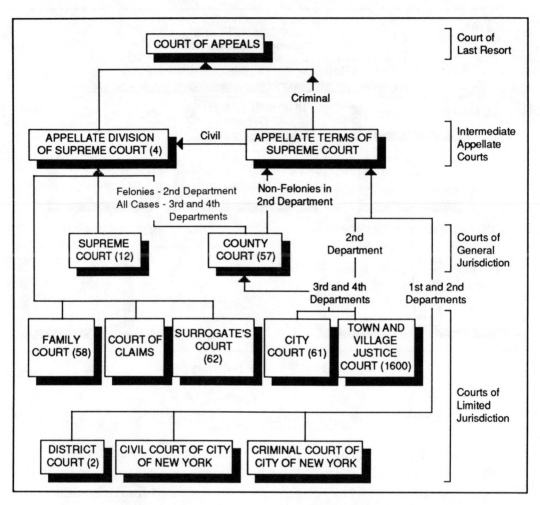

Figure 3-4: Present Route of Appeal in the New York State Court System

pellate Term to ease the division's case load. Appellate Terms have been established in large downstate urban and suburban areas in the First and Second Judicial Departments (see Figure 3-4). The Appellate Term hears civil and criminal appeals from local courts and certain appeals from County Courts. An Appellate Term consists of three to five Supreme Court justices. At least two justices must hear an appeal and concur in a decision.

COUNTY COURTS
In the Third and Fourth Judicial Departments, which have no Ap-

pellate Terms, the County Courts hear appeals from the local, city, town, and village courts. Appeals from the County Courts generally go to the Appellate Division of the Supreme Court.

State Trial Courts (Courts of Original Jurisdiction)

THE SUPREME COURT

The New York State Supreme Court is a court of original jurisdiction, which means that cases begin in that court. Although any type of case may begin in the Supreme Court, this court usually hears cases that are outside the jurisdiction of the specialized courts. In general, Supreme Court cases involve: civil matters dealing with monetary amounts above the jurisdiction of lower courts (e.g., negligence cases); divorce, separation, and annulment proceedings; and equity suits (e.g., mortgage foreclosures). In some large metropolitan areas, including New York City, the Supreme Court also hears felony prosecutions (e.g., prison sentences of one year or more).

Supreme Court decisions may be appealed to a higher court, either in an Appellate Division of the state's Supreme Court or the Court of Appeals, or both (see Figure 3-4).

THE COUNTY COURT

Every county outside of New York City has a County Court. County Courts handle criminal prosecutions, mostly for cases that could carry prison sentences of one year or more (felony). They also handle civil cases which involve monetary amounts up to $25,000.

THE FAMILY COURT

Every county, including the five counties of New York City combined as one, has a Family Court. This court handles many types of family problems, including:

- juvenile delinquency
- child protection, abuse, and neglect
- persons in need of supervision, or PINS (males under 16 and

females under 18 who are ungovernable or beyond the control of parents)

- review and approval of foster-care placements
- paternity determinations
- family offenses, including spouse abuse (a felony, which may be tried either in a criminal court or in Family Court)
- adoptions (concurrent jurisdiction with Surrogate's Court)
- support of dependent relatives
- termination of parental rights
- enforcement or modification of orders of support

Family Court does not handle cases involving divorce, separation, annulment proceedings, or, except on referral from Supreme Court, title to marital property.

Appeals from the Family Court go to the Appellate Division of the Supreme Court.

THE SURROGATE'S COURT

Every county in the state has a Surrogate's Court to hear cases involving deceased persons' affairs, such as the probate of wills and the administration of estates. Surrogate's Court shares concurrent jurisdiction with Family Court over adoptions. Appeals from the Surrogate's Court go to the Appellate Division of the Supreme Court.

THE COURT OF CLAIMS

The Court of Claims is a special trial court limited to trying claims against the state of New York. The court has headquarters in Albany and sits in various locations across the state. Appeals from the Court of Claims go to the Appellate Division of the Supreme Court.

Local Trial Courts (Courts of Original Jurisdiction)

Local courts outside New York City fall into four categories: District, Town, Village, and City Courts.

THE DISTRICT COURT

A District Court is created after a request by a local government(s) and approval of the voters in that area. Any county (except those in New York City), or any portion of a county consisting of contiguous towns/cities, may request a District Court as a local option. District Court jurisdiction extends to civil cases involving up to $15,000 and to criminal cases involving misdemeanors, violations, and offenses.

The state has only two District Courts, both in the Second Judicial Department. One is in Nassau County and the other in the western part of Suffolk County. District Court appeals generally are heard by the Appellate Term of the Supreme Court (see Figure 3-4).

TOWN AND VILLAGE COURTS

The jurisdiction of the Town and Village Courts in criminal cases includes misdemeanors and lesser offenses: violations carrying penalties of not more than 15 days in jail, and misdemeanors carrying penalties of 15 days to one year. Town and village courts can hear civil cases involving amounts up to $3,000.

The judges of these courts have the power to issue warrants for the arrest of people charged with crimes. The judges hold preliminary hearings and arraignments for those charged with more serious crimes and determine whether or not the accused should be released on their own recognizance (ROR), released on bail, or detained pending grand jury action. Appeals generally go to the County Courts in the 3rd and 4th Judicial Departments and to the Appellate Term of the Supreme Court in the 2nd Judicial Department.

CITY COURTS OUTSIDE NEW YORK CITY

City Courts exist in 61 cities and have criminal jurisdiction over misdemeanors and lesser offenses. Their civil jurisdiction covers a maximum of $15,000. Some City Courts have a small claims part for informal disposition of matters not exceeding $2,000 and/or a housing part for hearing housing violations an landlord/tenant disputes. The judges of these courts are empowered to issue warrants of arrest. Appeals generally go to the County Courts in the 3rd and 4th Judicial Departments and to the Appellate Term of the Supreme Court in the 2nd Judicial Department.

NEW YORK CITY COURTS

1. The Civil Court of the city of New York tries civil cases involving amounts up to $25,000. It also includes a small claims part with a $2,000 limit, and a housing part.

2. The Criminal Court of the city of New York conducts trials of misdemeanors (crimes with penalties of one year or less) and violations (penalties of 15 days or less). Criminal Court judges also act as magistrates, as do city, town, and village judges outside New York City.

Appeals go to the Appellate Term of the Supreme Court (see Figure 3-4).

JUDICIAL SELECTION

The state constitution mandates the methods for selecting judges. Some judges are elected and some are appointed. The issue of an appointive versus an elective judiciary has been controversial throughout the state's history.

In the state's early history, judges were appointed by a Council of Appointment. In 1821 the council was abolished, and the governor received power to appoint all judges with Senate confirmation. In 1846, however, New Yorkers, responding to the philosophy of Jacksonian democracy and weary of abuses stemming from landowners' control of the judiciary, abolished the system of appointed judges and established a completely elective judiciary. By 1894 boss control of nominations and elections prompted a partial return to the appointive system. The governor was given the power to appoint justices of the Appellate Division of the Supreme Court, and the mayor of New York City was given authority to appoint the city's Criminal Court judges. In 1949 the governor's appointive power was extended to the appointment, with Senate confirmation, of judges to the newly created Court of Claims. In 1962 the mayor of New York City was given the power to appoint judges of the Family Court in that city. Finally, a constitutional amendment approved in 1977 established a merit selection system for the governor's appointments of judges to the Court of Appeals.

Judges of the Supreme Court, County Court, Surrogate's Court, Family Court (except in New York City), New York City Civil Court, District Court, Town, and Village Courts are all elected by popular vote. With confirmation by the Senate, the governor appoints judges for the Court of Claims and fills vacancies on the Supreme, County, Surrogate's, and Family Courts until the next general election. Screening panels review qualifications and recommend candidates for judicial appointment. Although currently in use, screening panels for appointments are not mandated by the constitution.

Qualifications and Terms of Office

Judges and justices in New York State come to the bench in a variety of ways, depending on the court of service, and are subject to a variety of qualification requirements, lengths of service, and salaries.

JUDGES OF THE COURT OF APPEALS

The judges of the state's top court are appointed by the governor from candidates recommended by the Commission on Judicial Nomination. The appointments must be approved by the state Senate. The Commission on Judicial Nomination consists of 12 members serving four-year staggered terms. A quorum consists of 10 members. Four of its members are appointed by the governor, four by the Chief Judge of the Court of Appeals, and one each by the Speaker of the Assembly, the Temporary President of the Senate (Majority Leader), and the two legislative minority leaders. No more than six may be of the same political party, at least four (two each of the governor's and the Chief Judge's appointees) must not be lawyers, and none may be active judges. None may hold office in any political party, and all must be residents of the state.

The Commission on Judicial Nomination must be notified by the clerk of the Court of Appeals no later than eight months before a vacancy is to occur, or immediately in cases of death or resignation.

Two weeks before the vacancy, the commission must submit to the governor the names of seven people it considers well qualified for the position of Chief Judge. For the position of Associate Judge, it submits three to seven names. The governor makes the appointment from the names submitted, no sooner than 15 days and no later than 30 days after receiving them.

All of the commission's proceedings and records are confidential; only the governor has access to all of its information on the candidates recommended. The commission's final report is made public. Although all candidates must submit financial statements, only the financial statement of the person actually appointed is made public. Court of Appeals judges serve 14-year terms.

APPELLATE DIVISION JUSTICES

Supreme Court Justices are appointed to the Appellate Divisions by the governor. The governor also appoints a chief justice, called the Presiding Justice, in each division. The four presiding justices, with the Chief Judge of the Court of Appeals, constitute the Administrative Board which runs the day-to-day administration of the courts.

Presiding justices serve for the duration of their Supreme Court terms. The associate appellate justices serve for five years or for the remainder of their terms, whichever is shorter.

There are 24 appellate justice positions authorized by law. But if an appellate division certifies a need, the governor can appoint additional justices.

SUPREME COURT JUSTICES

Supreme Court justices are elected by the voters in the judicial district in which they serve. Candidates are nominated by Judicial District Conventions held by each political party, usually in mid-to-late-September of a year in which a Supreme Court post will become vacant. Sometimes the parties will cross endorse the same candidate, so the same name appears on two or more party lines on the ballot. Cross-endorsed candidates frequently have no opposition.

Supreme Court justices must have been members of the bar for at least 10 years. They serve 14-year terms or until age 70, whichever comes first.

COUNTY COURT JUDGES
County Court judges are elected by the voters in the county in which they serve after nomination by the county political parties. They must have been members of the bar for five years and residents of their county. They serve 10-year terms.

FAMILY COURT JUDGES
Family Court judges outside of New York City are elected by the voters of the county. They are nominated by the same process as County Court judges and must have been members of the bar for 10 years. They serve 10-year terms.

In New York City, Family Court judges are appointed by the mayor for 10-year terms.

SURROGATE'S COURT JUDGES
Surrogate's Court judges are also elected by the voters of the county in which they serve and are nominated in the same manner as County and Family Court judges. They serve 14-year terms in New York City and 10-year terms elsewhere. They must have been members of the bar for 10 years.

COURT OF CLAIMS JUDGES
The governor appoints, with Senate confirmation, judges to the Court of Claims for nine-year terms. Each must have been a member of the bar for at least 10 years.

DISTRICT COURT JUDGES
District Court judges are elected by the voters in their districts

following nomination by county political parties. They must be residents of their districts and members of the bar for at least five years. District Court judges serve six-year terms.

TOWN AND VILLAGE COURT JUSTICES
Town and Village Courts are the only courts that do not require justices to be members of the bar. Of approximately 2,400 Town and Village Court justices in New York State, most are not lawyers. Nonlawyers must take and pass an initial examination administered by the Office of Court Administration as well as attend an annual advanced course. Lawyers are required to attend annual advanced courses. Town and Village Court justices are elected for four-year terms.

CITY COURT JUDGES OUTSIDE NEW YORK CITY
City Court judges are either elected by the voters or appointed by local authorities. They must have been members of the bar for at least five years. Full-time judges serve 10-year terms; part-time judges serve six-year terms.

NEW YORK CITY CIVIL COURT JUDGES
Civil Court judges in New York City are elected for 10-year terms. They must have been members of the bar for at least 10 years.

NEW YORK CITY CRIMINAL COURT JUDGES
Criminal Court judges are appointed by the mayor of New York City for 10-year terms. They must have been members of the bar for at least 10 years.

Retirement of Judges and Justices

The state constitution requires that all state judges retire at age 70, except for Court of Appeals judges and Supreme Court justices who can serve on the Supreme Court and the Appellate Division up to six additional years if certified as physically and mentally fit.

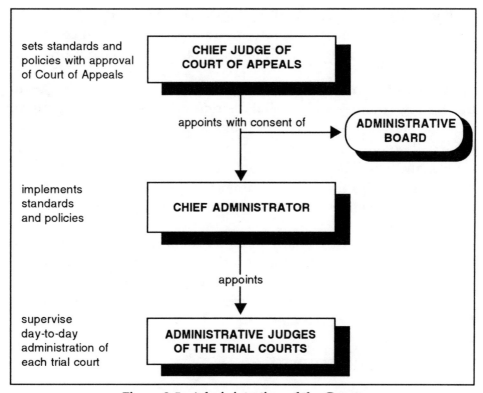

sets standards and
policies with approval
of Court of Appeals

**CHIEF JUDGE OF
COURT OF APPEALS**

appoints with consent of

**ADMINISTRATIVE
BOARD**

implements
standards
and policies

CHIEF ADMINISTRATOR

appoints

supervise
day-to-day
administration of
each trial court

**ADMINISTRATIVE JUDGES
OF THE TRIAL COURTS**

Figure 3-5: Administration of the Courts

COURT ADMINISTRATION

The state's court system is administered by the Chief Administrator, who is appointed by the Chief Judge of the Court of Appeals with the advice and consent of the Administrative Board. (If the Chief Administrator is a judge, the title of the office is Chief Administrative Judge.) On behalf of the Chief Judge, the Chief Administrator, as head of the Office of Court Administration, prepares the annual budgets of all courts of the unified court system, except for Town and Village courts; establishes terms of court and assigns judges to them; and generally regulates the flow of business in the courts (see Figure 3-5).

The Chief Administrator also is charged with hiring and supervising personnel, labor relations and collective bargaining with nonjudicial court employees, gathering and reporting statistical data, preparing legislative proposals to improve the efficiency of the courts, setting up continuing education programs for judges and court employees, and planning and developing court improvement projects.

The Chief Administrator's staff includes administrative judges in the various counties and judicial districts of the state, serving out of regional staff offices. The Chief Judge and the Chief Administrator are legally required to consult with the Administrative Board of the Courts and with the Judicial Conference. The Office of Court Administration helps the Chief Administrator run the courts, formulate rules, propose legislation, and produce official forms.

The Administrative Board is composed of the Chief Judge of the Court of Appeals and the four presiding justices of the Appellate Divisions. The Judicial Conference is composed of the above, plus judges who represent each of the trial courts and practicing lawyers from various parts of the state.

FINANCING THE COURTS

In 1976 the legislature adopted a Unified Court Budget Act which merged 120 separate court budgets into the state's judicial budget. The state also assumed responsibility for the operating costs of the courts, except for Town and Village Courts. By 1980 the state had assumed total funding of all operating costs of the courts, except for the Town and Village Courts which continue to be funded by their respective local governments.

While the state assumes responsibility for the operating costs of the courts, repair and maintenance of courthouses remain the responsibility of local governments. Statewide, court facilities have been deteriorating for many years because local funds were not committed for rehabilitation of the physical structures. In 1987 the legislature passed the court facilities bill to help local governments finance courthouse improvements. The New York State Dormitory Authority was authorized to issue up to $1.25 billion in bonds for courthouse construction and repair. A state fund, financed by increases in court user fees, reimburses a percentage of the interest on the loans for courthouse improvements and for the cost of maintaining the court facilities.

JUDICIAL DISCIPLINE

The New York State Commission on Judicial Conduct is the disciplinary agency designated by the constitution to review complaints of misconduct against judges of the state's unified court system.

The commission consists of 11 members who serve four-year staggered terms. Four are appointed by the governor, three by the Chief Judge of the Court of Appeals, and one each by the four leaders of the legislature. The constitution requires four members to be judges, at least one an attorney, and at least two nonlawyers. The commission elects one of its members as chairperson and appoints an administrator and a clerk who are in charge of day-to-day operations.

The types of complaints that may be investigated by the commission include: improper demeanor, conflicts of interest, intoxication, bias, prejudice, favoritism, gross neglect, corruption, certain prohibited political activity, and other misconduct on or off the bench.

Role of the Commission

The commission receives and reviews written complaints of misconduct against judges, initiates complaints, conducts formal hearings, subpoenas witnesses and documents, and makes determinations to dismiss or discipline. The commission does not make decisions related to judicial rulings of judges. Those decisions go through the appellate process. The commission is not expected to expose crimes, nor does it have the traditional powers of a prosecuting agency. After investigating and conducting a hearing, the commission may admonish, censure, remove a judge from office, or retire a judge for disability. The commission can also issue private, informal reprimands to deal with minor instances of judicial misbehavior. All of the commission's proceedings are confidential through the conclusion of the hearing. If the commission finds cause for disciplinary action against a judge, its findings are made available to the public through the office of the clerk of the Court of Appeals. The commission also publishes an annual report which is available to the public. Decisions of the commission may be appealed to the Court of Appeals, which can uphold, dismiss, reduce, or upgrade the disciplinary action. The commission is independent of the unified court system and is funded by the state legislature.

ATTORNEYS

A lawyer's special responsibilities in the administration of justice are to represent the interests of the client, to present evidence favorable to the client, and to enable the judge or the jury to reach a just decision. The lawyer safeguards the client's rights and interests throughout all phases of a trial.

The admission of attorneys to practice is carefully supervised. The New York State Board of Law Examiners, consisting of three lawyers appointed by the Court of Appeals, holds bar examinations twice each year for admission of attorneys. The names of those passing these tests are certified to the Appellate Divisions, which inquire into the character and fitness of candidates residing in their respective departments. Applicants are sworn in as attorneys and counsellors-at-law only after all of these requirements are satisfied.

All attorneys licensed to practice law in New York State are bound by the provisions of the Lawyer's Code of Professional Responsibility. Violations of the code can result in a range of disciplinary measures from a letter of caution to disbarment. There is a disciplinary panel that operates under the supervision of the Appellate Divisions of the State Supreme Court in each of the four judicial departments or regions.

Counsel for the Indigent

By state law the accused has the right to counsel at all stages of a criminal proceeding. If the accused is charged with a misdemeanor or felony and cannot afford counsel, the court must provide an attorney if the defendant requests one. In most cases, the judge decides whether or not the accused is entitled to free counsel. Court-provided counsel includes public defenders, private legal aid societies, and assigned counsel.

In civil matters, all parties in most Family Court proceedings, including children, have the right to an attorney. Attorneys appointed to represent children are known as law guardians. The court will usually assign a lawyer to a party who cannot afford one. Legal assistance for both parents also is provided in child support cases. Many agencies and programs provide civil legal representation for the poor.

THE JURY

Juries are an integral part of the due process of law in our courts. The jury system has also been called the "community arm of the courts" because it is the principal, and sometimes the only, contact citizens have with the courts. There are two kinds of juries in every county: the grand jury and the trial jury, sometimes called the petit jury.

The grand jury, composed of 16 to 23 people, is drawn from the same county jury pool as the trial jury. At least 16 jurors must be present at each meeting, and the agreement of 12 jurors is necessary to return an indictment. The grand jury has two functions—the indicting function and the investigative function. In its indicting function, the grand jury holds hearings and takes sworn testimony to determine if there is legally sufficient evidence to indict; that is, to hold for trial a person accused of a serious crime (felony, a crime punishable by a prison term of a year or more). If the grand jury finds the evidence insufficient, it hands down a "no true bill." If it finds that a person should be prosecuted for lesser charges (misdemeanors), it may direct the district attorney to do so.

The constitution guarantees that all people accused of felonies are entitled to grand jury hearings. The basis for this right is the belief that no one should be sent to trial unless there is some substantial foundation for the charge, as well as the belief that the grand jury hearing is the appropriate vehicle for screening these charges. Defendants accused of less than a Class A felony (punishable by 15 years to life incarceration) may waive the right to a grand jury hearing if the district attorney agrees, if the court is satisfied the waiver has been executed properly, and if a grand jury indictment has not already been handed down.

The district attorney is the sole legal adviser to the grand jury and subpoenas witnesses in the name of the grand jury. The grand jury may conduct investigations and bring indictments on its own initiative, but the more usual course is for the district attorney to present the evidence and request that an indictment be returned. Generally, the only evidence the grand jury hears is the case for the prosecution. The defense will be presented at the actual trial if an indictment is handed down. A grand jury never determines whether a person is, in fact, guilty. That is the function of the trial jury.

Witnesses appearing before the grand jury are automatically granted immunity from prosecution on any charges concerning the matter about which testimony is given. They are not entitled to counsel unless they waive this immunity. If a witness signs a waiver of immunity in front of the grand jury, he/she is entitled to counsel in an advisory capacity only.

All grand jury proceedings are held in secret. The only people present are the jurors, the district attorney, an administrative clerk, a stenographer, an interpreter (if necessary), the witness who is testifying, and, in certain cases, the attorney for the witness. The primary purpose of secret proceedings is to protect the witness from intimidation or harassment.

Other functions of the grand jury are to conduct investigations concerning the misconduct, nonfeasance, and neglect in public office by a public servant, whether criminal or not, and to take action with respect to such evidence as provided by law. Grand juries also may inquire into prison conditions.

Trial Juries—Civil and Criminal

Trial juries hear sworn testimony and decide questions of fact during a trial. A civil trial is a means of resolving a dispute between two parties. A broad range of subjects is covered by the civil law, including injury to personal property and breach of contract. Six-person juries decide civil cases, with agreement of five necessary for a verdict or judgment.

In criminal cases, individuals are prosecuted by the government, in the name of the people, for violating statutes that define particular crimes. The function of the jury is to decide if the facts are sufficient to establish guilt beyond a reasonable doubt.

Crimes are divided into two categories: felonies carrying a prison term of more than one year, and misdemeanors carrying a maximum sentence of one year. Crimes are further subdivided into degrees of seriousness. In felony cases, defendants are entitled to a jury of 12 persons; in misdemeanor cases, a jury of six persons. A unanimous verdict is necessary to convict a person of a crime.

The right to a trial by jury exists in most but not all types of cases. A right to trial by jury may be waived by the parties in a civil case or by the defendant in a criminal case, except for murder in the first degree.

Article 16 of the Judiciary Law lists qualifications, exemptions, and disqualifications for jury service. These are the same for trial jurors and grand jurors.

Qualifications: In order to qualify as a juror a person must:

1. be a citizen of the United States and a resident of the county
2. be not less than 18 years of age
3. not have a mental or physical condition which causes the person to be incapable of performing in a reasonable manner the duties of a juror
4. not have been convicted of a felony
5. be intelligent, of good character, able to read and write the English language with a degree of proficiency sufficient to fill out satisfactorily the juror qualification questionnaire, and be

able to speak the English language in an understandable manner. (Note: deaf and blind persons are not automatically excluded from jury duty.)

Disqualifications: Each of the following is disqualified from serving as a juror:

1. members in active service in the armed forces of the United States
2. elected federal, state, city, county, town, or village officers
3. heads of civil departments of federal, state, city, county, town, or village governments; a member of a public authority or state commission or board; secretary to the governor
4. federal judges or magistrates or a judge of the unified court system
5. persons who served on a grand or trial jury within the state, including in a federal court, within two years of the date of the next proposed service.

Although jury service is the civic responsibility of all qualified citizens, certain occupations disqualify, or exempt, persons from jury duty. New York State has one of the highest number of exemptions in the nation.

The Office of Court Administration has the ultimate responsibility for jury management. Each county has a commissioner of jurors, paid from the judiciary budget, who oversees the process of summoning and qualifying jurors. The commissioners also ensure that the courts in each county have an adequate number of qualified jurors who represent a cross section of the population.

A computer system in the Office of Court Administration provides all 62 counties with lists of potential jurors. This computer-generated, jury-call method combines three source lists into a single master list for each county, eliminates duplicate names, then randomly selects names of prospective jurors. The source lists include the names of those filing New York State income tax returns, licensed drivers, and registered voters. Persons may also volunteer to serve as jurors. Both grand and trial jurors are selected at random from the same master list of qualified jurors in each county.

DID YOU KNOW . . . that a parent who lives with and takes care of a child under age 16 may claim exemption from jury service?

State law permits Commissioners of Jurors, or the trial court, to excuse or postpone jury service to a future date of service if the date of summoning causes undue hardship or extreme inconvenience to the person called, a person under his/her care, or to the public. Approximately one million jury service summonses are sent out in New York State each year and half result in postponement requests that are usually granted.

Juror Fees

Juror fees are uniform in New York State. Jurors are paid a fee of $15 per day and an additional $6 per day for every day of attendance at a trial lasting more than 30 days. The juror fee is intended to help defray expenses incurred by jurors while fulfilling their civic duty, not to compensate for the work done.

Enforcement

Failure to respond to the juror qualification questionnaires and to jury summonses has been an increasingly serious problem in New York State. Nonresponse to summonses has been as high as 67 percent in some counties. Those who fail to respond can be fined up to $250 and face contempt-of-court penalties. These penalties can be imposed only after notice to the person called and a hearing before the court or a judicial hearing officer.

4.
THE LEGISLATIVE BRANCH*

The New York State Legislature is older than the United States Congress. Established as a law-making body in 1777 under the state's first constitution, it met first at Kingston before settling in Albany. Its size and composition have been altered repeatedly over the years, but it has remained a bicameral body with its two houses—the Senate and the Assembly—sharing equal powers.

After each federal census, in the year ending in a "2," a constitutionally mandated redistricting and reapportionment is carried out by a bipartisan joint committee of the legislature. The legislature remaps its own districts, 150 in the Assembly and a number in the Senate that may vary upward from 50. For the past several years, there have been 61 Senate districts. Prior to the 1982 Voting Rights Act amendments, districts were based almost exclusively on equal population standards. Note, however, that New York State must comply with the mandates of the Voting Rights Act of 1965 and the 1982 amendments that directly affect the redistricting efforts of states. These amendments are designed to prevent dilution of minority strength and to enhance minority access to the governing process. Under the 1982 provisions, public bodies may be obligated to draw boundary lines so as to create districts in which minority groups will be a majority of the eligible voters. Race and ethnicity are major factors in redistricting.

Other state directives for districting remain imbedded in the state

*By Deborah Wenig.

43

constitution, although they were largely superseded by the U.S. Supreme Court's "one-man, one-vote" decision more than 30 years ago.

POWERS AND LIMITATIONS OF THE LEGISLATURE

The New York State Legislature carries out three main functions:
policy-making, oversight, and representation.

Policy-Making

The legislature has the power to make laws in all areas excepting
those delegated to the federal government or reserved to the people.
It may:

- adopt programs affecting public health, safety, and welfare
- raise revenues
- regulate business
- create and abolish political subdivisions, grant them powers,
  and regulate their operations

In addition, it may establish its own districts and those from which
members of congress are elected. It may confirm, remove, and impeach public officials, and also propose amendments to the state and
federal constitutions.

This broad authority, however, is subject to some limits. Both the
federal and state constitutions prohibit legislation that infringes on
individual rights and liberties. The Home Rule Article, through provisions designed to protect local self-government, bars the legislature from passing laws that apply only to a single locality unless ex-
pressly requested to do so by the governing body of that community.
Nor can the legislature pass private or local bills changing the names
of persons, or locating or changing a county seat. The detailed nature
of the state constitution also places substantial limits on the
legislature's freedom to act in important areas of governmental concern, such as the raising and spending of public money and providing for public housing.

DID YOU KNOW . . . that the current New York State Constitution, ratified in 1894, is our fourth and is 80,000 words long, second in length only to Alabama?

One may view the legislature as a mediator in the conflicts among various interest groups within the state. It defines the state's priorities through the programs it enacts. Its tax laws determine how fiscal burdens of these programs shall be shared by the public and private sectors. Its appropriation decisions reflect public reaction to state programs and policies.

The legislative process is complicated by political factors in other ways. With the two houses frequently controlled by different parties, the minority in one house can generally count on its party majority in the other chamber to block action on major partisan issues. Impasses of this sort may hold up adjournment, may require the governor's intervention in working out a compromise, or may totally obstruct progress on a controversial matter.

As an independent branch of the state government, the legislature has the authority to make rules for its own proceedings, choose its own officers, and judge the election and qualifications of its own members. In order to permit the public to follow its deliberations, legislative sessions are open, and free debate is guaranteed by its rules. Statements made in the course of debate are "privileged" and may not form the basis of a libel suit or prosecution in any other tribunal.

Oversight

Legislators' responsibilities do not end with policy-making. They must engage in oversight of the laws that have been enacted, including:

- reviewing and evaluating actions of the governor
- overseeing administration of state programs
- approving state budgets

- approving executive appointments
- reviewing and renewing legislation

One way in which legislatures have attempted to increase their oversight function is through the use of "sunset laws" that mandate that agencies, programs, and policies be reviewed periodically for efficiency and effectiveness. Sunset laws establish an automatic expiration date. An independent evaluation is conducted and frequently testimony is heard by a joint committee of the legislature after which recommendations are made regarding the agency or program under review.

Representation

As a major function of the legislature, the individual legislators are responsible for representing the interests of their constituents. Much time is spent by the legislators providing a wide array of constituent services, ranging from responding to a letter about the recycling program in the state, to helping a citizen contact the correct person in the Department of Motor Vehicles, to posing for pictures with visiting school groups. Legislators must also be answerable for their voting record during their tenure in office.

THE LEGISLATORS

The men and women who exercise these broad legislative powers may come from any walk of life and represent any vocation or profession. For much of this century, lawyers dominated legislative ranks. In 1993 approximately 50 percent of the senators and 25 percent of the Assembly members were lawyers. Legislators are technically part-time officials, who may carry on private business or professions in addition to their legislative duties. Nearly three-fourths, however, list no other occupation but legislator. Many others give nearly full time to the demanding cycle of legislative business, constituent concerns, and campaign politics.

Terms for both senators and members of the Assembly are two years. Most legislators seek reelection; some stay in office for as long as 30 years. A member's length of service may be a factor in committee assignment, appointment to chairmanships, and general effectiveness. Periodically, four-year terms are suggested to potentially alleviate the constant need to be involved in campaign activities and fund-raising. Many argue that four-year terms would make legislators more responsive to constituents, rather than their large campaign donors, while others believe that the current two-year terms achieve the same goals of making legislators responsive to constituent concerns. As in many other states, recently there has been a call for term limits in New York State. Term limitations would require a constitutional amendment and approval by the electorate.

Members of the legislature must be citizens of the United States, residents of New York State for five years and of their Assembly or Senate district for one year prior to their election. While serving in the legislature, they may not hold any other elective office, except as a delegate to a constitutional convention; nor may they be appointed to any office that was created or had its salary increased during their legislative term.

Legislative salaries are fixed by law. Motivated by the political difficulty of raising their own salaries, the lawmakers adopted a measure in 1979 authorizing periodic future increases. Their salaries were $32,960 in 1983 and by 1993 were $57,500. In addition, legislators are entitled to per diems and are reimbursed for mileage expenses.

Legislative leaders, committee chairs, and ranking minority members of committees receive additional allowances. In practice, these leadership costs are distributed so that all senators and nearly half of the Assembly members receive extra compensation. Such compensation ranges from $6,500 to $30,000. This is the reason why it is possible for the average total salary for a state legislator to reach $79,000. Some examples of extra compensation for committee assignments are:

- Majority Whip of Senate: $16,000
- Chairman of Senate Labor Committee: $9,000

- Ranking minority member of Senate Labor Committee: $6,500
- Chair of Assembly Ways and Means Committee: $24,500
- Minority Whip of Assembly: $12,000

Every legislator is allotted office space. Leaders and a few major committee chairmen are accommodated in the Capitol Building; all others are across the street in the Legislative Office Building. In addition, members receive allowances for other offices in their home districts. The legislature also underwrites much of the cost of staff assistance, provides a bill drafting service, and maintains a research office to help members. Last, but not least, legislators are given allowances for printing and mailing newsletters to their constituents.

Legislative costs nearly tripled between 1979 and 1989, but have remained stable since. The legislative budget appropriation in Fiscal Year 1993-94 was $169.6 million.

SESSIONS OF THE LEGISLATURE

In contrast to other states, the New York State Legislature meets annually in limited session. It convenes at the New York State Capitol Building in Albany on the first Wednesday after the first Monday in January and continues in session until a date mutually agreed upon by both houses, usually around July 4th. Neither house may recess for more than two days without the consent of the other. Generally, legislators are in Albany three days a week but, as the session advances, they are likely to meet more often. In recent years, sessions have lasted for six months or longer. Since 1976 the legislature has declined to adjourn formally when its work is completed. This permits its members to return on short notice to take up a special issue or overturn a veto. Some see the open-ended sessions as a step toward a full-time legislature.

Special sessions, called extraordinary sessions, may be called by the governor. At such times, the legislature may act only on matters that the governor has put before it. However, in the absence of formal adjournment, the legislature can now return to regular session and its own agenda at any time, which considerably weakens the governor's control. Once a rare occurrence, special sessions have been used increasingly to address unfinished business.

Under a 1975 constitutional amendment, to date unused, the legislature may also be convened by its leaders if they have been petitioned by two-thirds of the members. Only subjects enumerated in the petition may then be on the session agenda. The legislature is also automatically convened by notice from the Chief Judge of the Court of Appeals, if charges for removal or retirement have been brought against a judicial officer.

The legislature holds joint sessions—with both houses sitting together in the larger Assembly Chamber—to receive the governor's annual "State of the State" message and for the election of members of the New York State Board of Regents.

The session is only the more visible part of legislative work. During the rest of the year, the lawmakers perform various services for their constituents, serve on committees and commissions developing legislation, or even gather informally in "mini-sessions" to make plans for the coming session.

ORGANIZATION OF THE LEGISLATURE

The functioning of the legislature can be understood best in political terms. Legislators almost always belong to one of the two major political parties, although occasionally a legislator enrolled as Conservative, Liberal, or Right to Life receives a Democratic or Republican endorsement. Because majority and minority members sit on opposite sides of the Senate and Assembly chambers, a legislator will frequently refer to the opposition party as "the other side of the aisle."

Before the opening session, each party caucuses to select its nominees for officers of the Senate or Assembly. It is important to note that since legislation was passed in 1985 deliberations of the party caucuses are closed to the public. At times, dissension within a party has caused a contest over the leadership. Once that matter is decided, each party votes as a bloc on the organization of the legislature. This procedure gives the majority party in each house the ability to name its officers and make the rules. Majority leaders then exercise effective control by making appointments, thus ensuring that their members chair and dominate all committees with sufficient votes to pass or defeat measures. In effect, this means that minority members of each house can usually obtain passage of minor bills, but can only cosponsor significant legislation with the majority party.

At the opening session in January after the oath of office has been administered, the newly elected members formally organize by voting on the decisions that have already been made in their pre-session caucuses. At that time they also adopt rules that will govern their procedures for the two-year term. In either house the rules may be amended at any time.

THE OFFICERS

The presiding officer of the Senate is the lieutenant-governor, who serves by virtue of his office, and who may not join the debate or vote on any question except to break a tie. Political control belongs to the majority leader.

Each party nominates a candidate to serve as Temporary President of the Senate, commonly referred to as the majority leader. The unsuccessful candidate becomes the minority leader. The majority leader has general supervision over the business of the Senate and appoints the chair and members of all committees, as well as most of the administrative and auxiliary employees. The majority and minority leaders are generally the spokespersons for their parties and are responsible for shepherding their bills through the legislative process.

In the Assembly, the presiding officer is the speaker, elected by the members upon the nomination of the majority party. The speaker is the center of power in the Assembly, directing the course of its business, ruling on parliamentary procedure, and certifying the passage of all bills. The speaker may leave the chair to debate on any measure, although it is rarely done, and may vote even if not required to do so except to break a tie. The speaker makes all committee assignments and appoints and directs the work of most of the Assembly staff.

The speaker's first official act is to appoint the majority leader of the Assembly, who is floor manager for his/her party's legislative proposals. The minority leader performs duties similar to those of the minority leader of the Senate.

As soon as both houses are organized, each sends a select committee, consisting of a member from each party, to inform the governor that they are ready to proceed with business and will meet in joint session to receive the annual message. The present custom is for the governor to deliver a message personally in the Assembly Chamber on the first day of the session. In the "State of the State" address, the governor reports on developments since the last session and recommends matters for attention during the new one. This annual message is a blueprint of the governor's legislative program that will be developed more fully in the budget message. After receiving the governor's message, the senators return to their own chamber, and the legislative session is officially underway.

THE COMMITTEES

Much of the work of the legislature takes place in its standing committees. The Senate Majority Leader and Assembly Speaker, in consultation with the minority leaders, appoint the members of these committees. Although seniority and the prestige of an individual legislator will influence their assignment, no fixed pattern or precedent governs the appointments. In all cases, the chair and a majority of committee members belong to the majority party.

Every bill begins (and sometimes ends) its progress through the legislature in one of these committees. No bill reaches the floor of either house for debate unless it has been "reported out" to the floor by a standing committee. But in many cases, a committee will refer its important measures not to the floor but to the rules or finance committees (Assembly Ways and Means or Senate Finance) of their respective houses, where leadership control resides.

Rules Committee

The key committee in each house is the Rules Committee; the Senate Majority Leader and Assembly Speaker serve as the respective chairpersons in both the Senate and Assembly. The membership of the Rules Committee is made up of the chair and ranking minority members of other important standing committees. These committees should not be confused with congressional committees of the same name that adopt a "rule" for each measure to determine when and how it may be debated.

The chief power of the Rules Committee in the state legislature is the forum it affords for leadership decision-making. For the most part, bills that lack support of these few key legislators do not pass. Many of the formal procedures through which this power was once exercised have been changed and the autocratic image of the leaders modified, but the center of control is essentially unaltered. For example, Assembly standing committees are no longer required to report out all of their bills on a date set by the speaker, but they continue voluntarily to transfer their most controversial business to the Rules Committee as the recess approaches. In the Senate, the committee has authority to take over bills referred to any other committee, but it rarely does so. Late in the session, after a compromise has been finally negotiated on a troublesome issue, only the Rules Committees have the ability to get the accepted version to the floor for action, for these committees alone may introduce bills after the deadlines for individual introductions have passed.

The ability to determine the order in which bills are presented for a vote is another critical function of leadership, exercised as the session advances. Hundreds of measures just do not get into print until after the session has ended, in part because of the huge print backlog, but also because of their low priority to the leadership.

Finance Committee

The Finance Committee, which has an input in any bill involving expenditure of state money, is the second significant repository of leadership control. Important measures that are not referred to Rules are most often reported to the Finance Committee in the Senate, and to the Ways and Means Committee in the Assembly. The chairs of committees that forward their bills in this manner are often members of either the Finance or the Rules Committees themselves.

Standing Committees

In 1994 there were 32 standing committees in the Senate and 36 in the Assembly. Assembly committees generally have 18 to 22 members but can range from seven to 38. Senate committees are usually smaller, ranging from seven to 23.

Most senators serve on six standing committees, members of the Assembly on three or four. Overlapping responsibility is built into the system. Few committees can expect full attendance at all meetings, but they do meet regularly and give independent consideration to their assigned bills. Some say committee performance has been enhanced by the presence of the press and public. Unless two-thirds of the members vote for a closed session, all committee meetings are now open.

In spite of its large number of standing committees, the legislature appoints other groups to develop legislative proposals and policies. Among them are some permanent legislative commissions with both Senate and Assembly members. These have continuing responsibilities, such as the Commission on Expenditure Review and the Bill Drafting Commission.

Others are temporary joint legislative commissions, created by statute, or task forces created by resolution for a specific purpose and a limited term. Some may include nonlegislative members. All may hire staff, may give intensive attention to an issue outside the pressures and politics of the session, and may produce legislative recommendations. None, however, may introduce bills.

Each house also has its own select committees or task forces addressing issues that do not easily fit into a standing committee's jurisdiction. Examples are:

- Senate Task Force on Drunk Driving
- Assembly Task Force on Food, Farm, and Nutrition
- Assembly Task Force on Women's Issues
- Assembly Task Force on the Disabled

5.
HOW A BILL BECOMES A LAW*

A legislative proposal introduced in the Senate or Assembly is called a bill. To become a law, a bill must be passed in exactly the same form by both houses and then signed by the governor. If vetoed, the bill can become law only by a two-thirds vote of both houses.

DID YOU KNOW . . . that only about 5 percent of bills introduced become laws?

At the legislative session of 1920, 3,442 bills were introduced. Of these, nearly 27 percent, or 940, were signed into law or chaptered. Seventy-three years later, the number of measures presented to the legislature reached well over 14,000, but the number of bills signed into law amounted to 731.

The vast increase in introductions reflects expanded activities of the state as well as a rise in the number of politically active lobbying groups, each with its own legislative objectives. It also represents duplication. This duplication often occurs because each legislator wants to gain credit for sponsoring bills that are politically popular or requested by a constituent or special interest group. Thus, a large number of closely similar bills are introduced year after year without much prospect for passage. The volume is so great that few, if any, legislators can successfully follow all the bills during the legislative session. As seen by the numbers above, relatively few measures survive the pitfalls and complexities that surround each step in

*By Evelyn Stock, with acknowledgment to *The Citizen Lobbyist.*

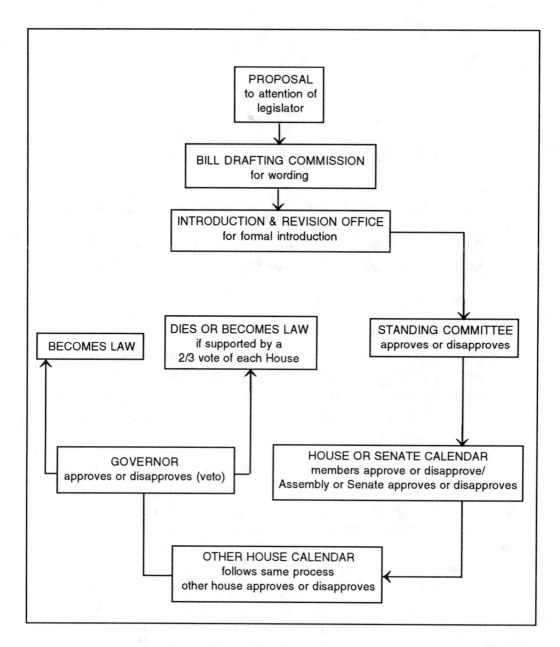

Figure 5-1: How a Bill Becomes a Law

this process (see Figure 5-1).

WHO MAY INTRODUCE BILLS

Bills may be introduced in a number of ways:

- by a member or members of either house (most bills are introduced this way)
- by report of a standing committee or by the Rules Committee in either house
- by order of either house (rare)
- by message from either house (when one house passes a bill, it is sent to the other house for action)
- by message from the governor (budget bills only)

The idea behind a particular bill can be initiated by a private citizen, an organization, a professional association, a government official, an individual legislator, a legislative committee, or the governor. Much program legislation is proposed by the governor or by one of the executive departments or agencies. These are referred to as program bills. Anyone may actually draft legislation and ask a legislator to introduce it.

Multi-sponsored bills are sponsored by two or more legislators in the same house. Companion bills are identical bills cosponsored by one or more members of the Assembly and one or more senators in the Senate. Uni-bills are printed only once and simultaneously introduced into both houses; the names of both their Senate and Assembly sponsors appear on the measure.

SCHEDULE FOR INTRODUCING BILLS

Legislators may prefile bills between November 15 and the opening of the session. Considered introduced on the first day of the session, prefiled bills are printed and ready for committee consideration when the legislature convenes. In both houses, members may introduce an unlimited number of bills during January and February; members are then limited in the number of new introductions

STATE OF NEW YORK

8870

1993-1994 Regular Sessions

IN ASSEMBLY

July 7, 1993

Introduced by COMMITTEE ON RULES -- (at request of M. of A. Brodsky, We-
prin, Silver, Grannis, DiNapoli, Englebright, Meeks, Stringer, Bar-
baro, Brennan, Cahill, Clark, Colman, Cook, Davis, Del Toro, Feldman,
Jenkins, Koppell, Matusow, Mayersohn, Pretlow, Rivera, Sanders, Tal-
lon, Towns, Weisenberg, Straniere, Parola) -- (at request of the Governor) -- read once and referred to the Committee on Ways and Means

AN ACT to amend the environmental conservation law, the economic
development law, the vehicle and traffic law, the public lands law,
the tax law, the state finance law, the real property tax law and
chapter 57 of the laws of 1993 amending the tax law relating to income
tax rates and deductions, in relation to creating the environmental
protection act and repealing article 54 of the environmental conservation law, relating thereto

The People of the State of New York, represented in Senate and Assembly, do enact as follows:

1   Section 1. Short title. This act shall be known as the "environmental
2 protection act".
3   § 2. Legislative findings and declaration. The legislature hereby
4 finds, declares, and reaffirms that the preservation, enhancement,
5 restoration, improvement and stewardship of the state's environment are
6 among the government's most fundamental obligations; and that appropri-
7 ate actions to make the state's invaluable natural and historic
8 resources available for public use and enjoyment are key components of
9 the environmental and social policy of the state.
10   The legislature further finds and declares that it is imperative that
11 actions be taken now so that the state will enter the twenty-first cen-
12 tury with an environmentally sound and effective program for managing
13 solid waste. This includes comprehensive planning as well as the imple-

EXPLANATION--Matter in _italics_ (underscored) is new; matter in brackets
[ ] is old law to be omitted.

LBD11418-22-3

until the end of the session. The deadlines are set by each house each year. After the deadline, only the Rules Committees may introduce bills unless introductory numbers were reserved for bills under preparation by individual legislators. However, a legislator elected after the deadline is given some opportunity to introduce bills.

THE PROGRESS OF A BILL

Bills may be introduced in either or both houses. When introduced, a bill is said to be on "First Reading." ("First Reading," "Second Reading," and "Third Reading" are terms dating from the time each bill was read aloud in full in public session three times before final action could be taken.) The bill is put into printed form and is assigned a print number in the order in which it is introduced. This number identifies it as the bill moves through the year's legislative process. An "A" preceding the bill number designates an Assembly bill, and an "S" preceding the bill number designates a Senate bill. All bills carry the title of the bill, the introducer's name and a brief description. The sponsor prepares a memorandum to accompany the bill, describing its purpose. If a bill is amended, a letter is added to the number (e.g., Senate bill S.138 becomes S.138A), and the bill is reprinted as amended with the amended number. Each time a bill is amended, it is reprinted with its original print number; amended versions are denoted by a letter suffix: A, B, C, D, E, etc. each time the bill is amended. If a bill is amended in the other house, it receives a separate print number.

DID YOU KNOW . . . that most bills die in committee?

The leader of each house assigns all bills to an appropriate standing committee. It is here that much of the work of the legislature is done. Except under very special circumstances, no bill is taken up for debate or a vote on the floor of the house, unless it has received a majority of the votes in committee and has been reported out (sent) to the floor by the leadership. Before recommending a bill for passage, a committee may hold public hearings. A bill that is voted down in committee is considered "dead" for the session. Generally, the device used to stop or "kill" a bill is a vote to "hold the bill in committee." In the Assembly, the sponsor can request that the committee consider the bill. In the Senate, chairs of committees can refuse to consider particular bills. Early in the session, a legislator may make a motion to "discharge from the committee" a bill stalled in committee so that it will be brought to the Assembly floor for consideration.

Once a bill is reported out of committee, it appears on the "Second Reading Calendar" in the Assembly or "Order of First Report" in the Senate. A bill cannot receive final action until it has been moved to the "Third Reading Calendar." Each house prints a daily calendar that serves as an agenda for legislative sessions and contains those measures that have come through the committees.

No bill may be passed until it has been on the legislators' desks in printed form for three legislative days. However, this requirement is waived if the governor sends a Message of Necessity to the legislature indicating that the bill should be considered at once. Even with the Message of Necessity, a bill must be on legislators' desks in final, although not necessarily printed, form before it can receive action. A bill that appears on the calendar with an "H" (for High Print) next to its number is not ready for a final vote because it has not been on the desks in finished form for the required time. Toward the end of the session, it is not uncommon for legislators' desks to be covered with stacks of bills two feet high.

OBSTACLES TO THE PROGRESS OF BILLS

The leadership is the traffic manager for getting measures to the floor, but much may happen to a bill even after it appears on a third reading.

DID YOU KNOW . . . that a star next to a bill can actually kill it?

A bill may be stopped in the Assembly at the third reading stage if the introducer (in the Senate, it is the Majority Leader) places a star next to its calendar listing. A starred bill cannot advance until 24 hours after the star is removed. Most sessions adjourn with hundreds of starred bills still on their calendars.

A bill may be amended any time until its third reading. Actually, even after it has been passed, it can be amended by motion to reconsider the vote by which it passed. It can even be recalled from the governor's desk after it has passed both houses. Every session sees some of these recalls.

When a bill passes one house, it is sent to the other, where it goes through an identical process. A bill may be amended in either house and returned to the other house for concurrence with the amendment. Sometimes, the Senate and Assembly pass measures that are similar but not identical. Since there is no conference (as there is in Congress) to resolve differences, it is possible for each house to pass its own version of a controversial or politically sensitive measure, then place the blame on the other house for failure to act.

Some bills that have not been acted on by the end of the first year of a two-year term of a legislature are carried over and considered to be automatically introduced without reprinting in the second year.

PASSING THE BILLS

Most bills that get as far as a vote are noncontroversial and pass with very little dissent by members of either party. Relatively few measures are ever presented for full floor debate. Positions on important bills are usually reached at party conferences (caucuses of all legislators of each party), where the leaders exert great influence. Legislators persistently voting in opposition to their parties can find themselves with poor committee assignments and lack of party support for their own measures.

COUNTING THE VOTE

A constitutional quorum must be present in the Senate or Assembly when a final vote on any bill is taken. In the case of most legislation, a quorum is a simple majority (one more than half) of all the elected members. Three-fifths of the members are needed for a quorum if a bill imposes, continues, or revises a tax; creates a public debt; or appropriates public money.

Most bills can be passed by a simple majority of the total membership of the house. A two-thirds majority is required to pass certain home rule bills (bills which appropriate public money or property for private or local purposes) and to override the governor's veto.

After disposing of the noncontroversial bills, the house turns to the controversial measures. If there is to be debate, the time allotted each member is limited. No one may speak more than twice on the same bill on the same day.

The constitution requires that the ayes and nays on every bill be recorded in a journal of proceedings. On noncontroversial measures, this record is accomplished through the "fast roll call," which means that the clerk reads the first and last name on the alphabetical list of members and the names of the majority and minority leaders. All present are presumed to have voted in favor of the bill. (In the Assembly, presence is recorded through an electronic attendance system.) Members may be recorded in opposition by raising their hands during fast roll call.

Fast roll calls often take place when the majority or minority leader indicates there will be a party vote on a bill. In that case, members are recorded as voting according to party affiliation, unless they indicate a wish to be recorded with the opposition. Fifteen members in the Assembly and five in the Senate may force a "slow roll call," in which the vote of every member of the house is individually recorded. Votes on controversial measures are almost always taken by slow roll call.

In the final weeks or days of the session, a special calendar called the Rules Calendar appears. This is the action list. The bills on it represent the compromises that have been worked out in leadership councils. Many of these measures are accompanied by a Message of Necessity from the governor to hasten passage.

ACTION BY THE GOVERNOR

A bill may be sent to the governor when it has passed both houses. Upon receipt of the bill, the governor is given 10 days to act on it. Bills sent within 10 days of the end of the session must be acted on within 30 days after the last day of the session. Since final action is taken on most bills during the last two weeks, this 30-day bill-signing period is inevitably a very busy time.

In recent years, the legislature has recessed instead of adjourning when its major business is done. Technically, this does not give the governor the 30-day constitutional period that ordinarily would be needed to deal with the session's output. In practice, however, the legislature has delayed sending some of the bills, delivering them instead over a period of weeks to allow a reasonable time to consider the huge number of measures passed in the final days.

If the governor takes no action on a 10-day bill, it automatically becomes a law. If the governor disapproves or vetoes a 10-day bill, it can become law only if it is repassed or "overridden" by two-thirds vote in each house. If the governor fails to act on a 30-day bill, the bill is said to have received a "pocket veto." It is customary for the governor to act, however, on all bills submitted and to give reasons in writing for approving or disapproving important legislation.

CONSTITUTIONAL AMENDMENTS

Proposed amendments to the New York State Constitution, or ratification of proposed amendments to the United States Constitution, are introduced as Concurrent Resolutions in both houses. They follow a path similar to that of ordinary legislation, except that no action by the governor is necessary.

A proposed amendment to the New York State Constitution is acted on only after it has been referred to the attorney general for an opinion as to its effect on other provisions of the constitution. It must be passed by two separately elected (but consecutive) legislatures, with the second passage effected in the first regular session of a legislature's two-year term. It is then presented to the voters for approval at a general election. If approved, it takes effect in January following the referendum.

6.
STATE FINANCES*

BUDGET-MAKING

The New York State Constitution provides for a strong executive budget. This requires the governor to prepare a comprehensive plan for the state each fiscal year, showing both a plan of disbursements (spending) to implement proposals and an estimate of the receipts (income) that will be available to support these disbursements. Through this budget-making procedure, the governor is the chief architect of the state's policies and programs. Annual consideration of the budget is the legislature's most important business. The governor can exercise an item veto on any appropriation initiated by the legislature throughout the session.

The governor is not entirely a free agent in developing financial plans, but is limited by restrictions in the state constitution on the way money may be spent. These include prohibitions against the gift or loan of state monies or credit to private undertakings. However, the constitution lists many exceptions to this rule, allowing the state to support certain enterprises that provide aid to special classes of dependent citizens, or that promote state responsibilities in such specified fields as education, health, welfare, and retirement benefits. In addition, the governor must ask for specific voter authorization on every state bond issue, although other forms of borrowing, discussed later, do not require such a vote.

*Special thanks to the New York State Division of the Budget for budget figures and charts, Ruth Goldstein, and Nancy Callahan.

Within these restrictions and under the governor's direction, the Division of the Budget in the executive department prepares the budget. In preparing it, each department submits its appropriation request to the Division of the Budget by mid-September for the coming fiscal year (April 1 to March 31). In late September, the division begins its analysis and evaluates these requests in detail. Both the legislature and the Chief Judge of the Court of Appeals submit estimates of their operating expenses to the governor who must insert these in the budget as presented.

Data from the Department of Taxation and Finance and from the Office of the State Comptroller assist the Division of the Budget in projecting the state's receipts for the coming fiscal year. The division also prepares detailed economic forecasts of both the United States and New York State. By mid-January a completed budget reflecting the governor's policies is ready for presentation.

The governor must submit a budget to the legislature by the second Tuesday after the opening of the legislature (mid-January), and by February 1 in each year after a governor is elected. With its submission, the governor delivers a budget message containing the broad outlines of program proposals and plans for new taxes or other sources of receipts. Specific legislation that will implement these proposals is introduced in the form of budget bills.

The legislature must act on the appropriation bills submitted by the governor before considering any other appropriation bills. It may strike out or reduce, but may not increase, the appropriations recommended in the governor's budget. It may add items, provided each is "stated separately and distinctly" and refers to a single object or purpose.

The governor does not sign and cannot veto legislative action on budget items originated in the executive department. Appropriations for the legislature and judiciary, and separate items added to the budget by the legislature, are subject to the governor's approval or veto.

This system results in a good deal of give and take between the governor and the legislature. The governor prepares the budget and recommends methods of financing it. If the legislature disapproves of the methods advocated, the burden falls on the legislature to decide which programs will be curtailed to reduce disbursements, or to propose alternative means of financing. If it wishes to add new items, it may create additional sources of receipts, but the governor must agree to these.

Both courses—curtailing of programs and adding new resources—are frequently unpopular with the public. A political settlement must be reached between the governor and legislative leaders. In recent years, the influence of the legislature in the budget-making process has grown due to the ability of its fiscal committees to develop independent evaluations and forecasts of receipts and disbursements. In fact, in the 1980s some of the most significant budgetary actions, including the 1987 Tax Reform Act, originated in these fiscal committees.

Despite the legislature's heightened fiscal sophistication, it is often difficult for its leaders to muster the votes necessary for a budget accommodation with the governor. Coalitions of suburban legislators may be protecting aid to education, while urban representatives or caucuses of minority groups may be bargaining on social welfare programs. Or individual legislators may be using their votes to bargain over a "conscience" issue, such as abortion or capital punishment. Such interests sharply challenge the party discipline that leaders need to negotiate successfully with the governor.

The state's fiscal year ends on March 31, requiring a new budget to be adopted before April 1. In the past decade, various crises have caused the legislature to delay adoption of the budget for periods ranging from several days to a few months, but more recent policy outlines have been approved in April with the fine-tuning of political settlements occurring in May and June before the close of the legislative session. These are usually reflected in a "joint clean-up" budget bill, which the governor works out with the legislature in the closing days of the session, usually in early July.

After the budget has been adopted, programs or agencies may

Table 6-1
STATE RECEIPTS (TEN-YEAR GROWTH)
GENERAL FUND
(in $ millions)

	1983-84 actual	1993-94 actual	$ change	% change
PERSONAL INCOME	9,417	16,033	6,616	1
USER TAXES AND FEES	5,301	6,296	995	0
Sales and use	3,757	4,560	803	0
Motor fuel	396	174	(222)	(1)
Cigarette	438	708	270	1
Motor vehicle fees	418	450	32	0
Alcoholic beverage taxes and fees	234	246	12	0
Highway use	58	11	(47)	(1)
Other	0	147	147	
BUSINESS TAXES	2,808	5,882	3,074	1
Corp. franchise	1,201	1,948	747	1
Corp. and utilities	929	1,592	663	1
Insurance	213	636	423	2
Banks	172	851	679	4
Other	293	855	562	2
OTHER REVENUES	590	1,123	533	1
Real property gains	158	93	(65)	(0)
Estate and gift	259	799	540	2
Real estate transfer	59	163	104	2
Pari-mutuel	113	67	(46)	(0)
Other	1	1	0	0
MISCELLANEOUS	957	1,245	288	0
TOTAL REVENUES	19,073	30,579	11,506	1

encounter cost overruns. These must be covered by deficiency appropriations. Such appropriations may add to a previously authorized appropriation that has expired or is expected to be inadequate. Early in each session before the fiscal year ends, the legislature acts on a deficiency budget designed to carry the state's programs and departments through the remainder of the fiscal year.

Prior to 1981, the state's budgetary practices had been criticized from an accounting standpoint. However, the Accounting, Financial Reporting and Budget Accountability Report Act of 1981 introduced a new dimension to New York State's financial accounting and reporting practices—the use of Generally Accepted Accounting Principles (GAAP). With the enactment of this reform, the governor now presents his Financial Plan and Executive Budget both on the traditional "cash" basis and in accordance with GAAP. State accounting and financial reporting are also required to be in accordance with these principles.

Also, as a result of the 1981 legislation, beginning in 1983 the state moved to an "all funds" budget, greatly increasing the scope of the state's financial plan. Included in "all funds" are the General Fund, Special Revenue Funds, Capital Projects Funds, and Debt Service Funds. Special Revenue Funds account for state receipts from specific revenue sources and are legally restricted to disbursements for specified purposes. This fund type includes federal funds and state funds. The Capital Projects Funds account for capital construction costs. Debt Service Funds account for the payment of principal and interest on general obligation long-term debt, lease-purchase, and other contractual obligations.

GENERAL FUND RECEIPTS AND DISBURSEMENTS

Unlike the United States Constitution, the New York State Constitution requires the governor to offer a balanced budget; that is one in which receipts are sufficient to meet the proposed disbursements. Most of the income for the General Fund budget comes from current receipts derived primarily from taxes and fees (see Figures 6-1 and 6-2).

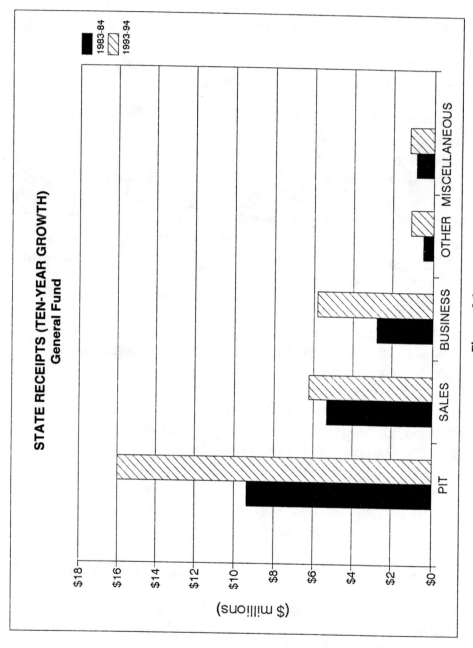

Figure 6-1

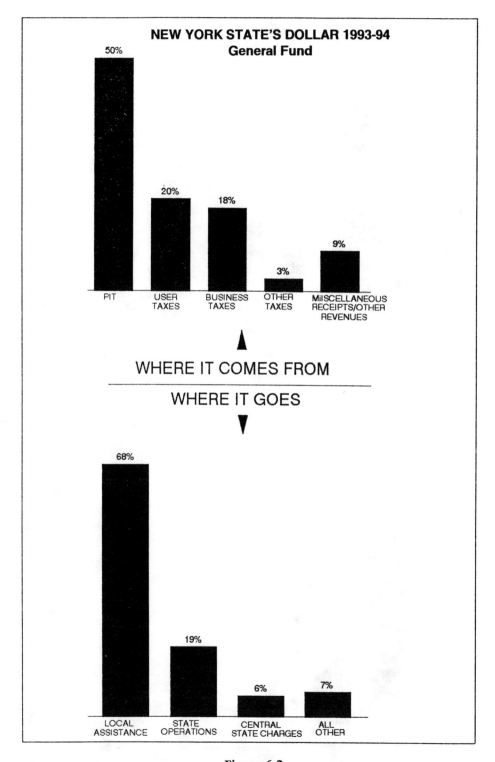

Figure 6-2

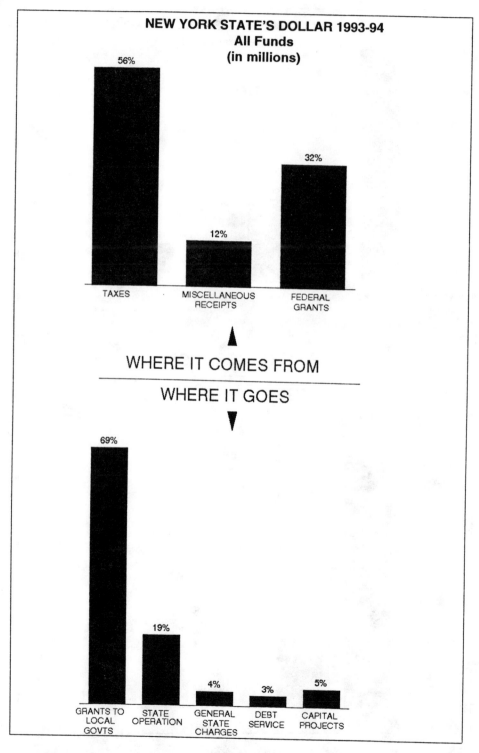

Figure 6-3

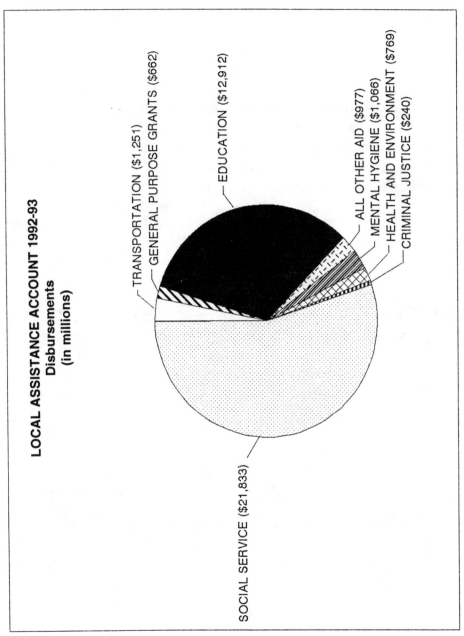

LOCAL ASSISTANCE ACCOUNT 1992-93
Disbursements
(in millions)

TRANSPORTATION ($1,251)
GENERAL PURPOSE GRANTS ($662)
EDUCATION ($12,912)
ALL OTHER AID ($977)
MENTAL HYGIENE ($1,066)
HEALTH AND ENVIRONMENT ($769)
CRIMINAL JUSTICE ($240)
SOCIAL SERVICE ($21,833)

Figure 6-4

The monies from these sources are disbursed in five principal ways (see Figure 6-3):

1. *Grants to Local Governments.* In fiscal year 1992-93, this accounted for 68 percent of the General Fund budget and went primarily to aid local governments and school districts. Much of it was designated for specific programs in social services, education, health, and mental hygiene, but a major portion was allocated through formulas for school aid and for unrestricted aid to localities (see Chapter 7).

2. *State Operations.* In fiscal year 1992-93, this group accounted for over 19 percent of General Fund disbursements. It paid for the staff and activities of state departments and agencies and is often called "the operating budget."

3. *General State Charges.* These costs which accounted for almost 7 percent of the General Fund budget are mandated either by statute, collective bargaining agreement, or court order. The major portion of appropriations in this area funds fringe benefits for employees. A smaller segment funds fixed costs, including payments in lieu of taxes and judgments against the state.

4. *Debt Service.* Less than 1 percent of the General Fund budget reflects the interest costs to the state on short-term borrowing.

5. *Transfers to Other Funds.* This category includes spending from the General Fund for capital projects, debt service on long-term bonds, and subsidies to certain state programs. It accounts for 5 percent of the General Fund budget.

WHAT THE BUDGET PAYS FOR

The presentation of the entire budget, known as "all-funds," provides a complete picture of state income and spending by category (see Figure 6-3). Total state income includes revenue from all sources— taxes, federal aid, fees, and bond proceeds. However, the distribution of General Fund spending provides the best indicator of state priorities since it primarily reflects the spending of tax dollars (see Figure 6-2). Of total General Fund spending, more than 68 percent, or $21.1 billion, is in the form of aid to localities.

Figure 6-4 shows how General Fund "assistance to local governments" is distributed by function. Some of the major activities included in the categories named in Figure 6-4 are:

1. *Education.* Includes state aid to local school districts; support for community colleges and the State University of New York (SUNY); state contributions to private institutions of higher learning and to the City University of New York (CUNY); tuition assistance payments to students.

2. *General Purpose Aid.* Payments to cities, towns, and villages for the support of local governments.

3. *Health and Social Development.* Income assistance and medical assistance for those who do not meet minimum standards of income; supplements federal aid for dependent children; aid for local health departments; support for facilities for treatment of tuberculosis, cancer, physical handicaps, and sexually transmitted diseases; research into cancer detection, kidney ailments, and birth defects; monitoring occupational health hazards; and programs for the aging.

4. *Mental Hygiene.* Facilities for treatment of mental illness, addiction, and mental retardation.

5. *Public Protection.* Crime control programs; probation and rehabilitation services.

6. *Transportation.* Support for public transportation systems (primarily the Metropolitan Transportation Authority).

All state payments are made through appropriations (authorization to spend) which do not always coincide with disbursements (actual expenditure) since less than the full appropriation may happen to be spent within the time authorized. The unspent part then can no longer be used. If the unspent balance has been specifically committed, it may be used up to three months (for state operations and general state charges) and five and a half months (for all other categories) after the close of the fiscal year. Because capital projects usually take more than one fiscal year to complete, reappropriations are often necessary to complete projects started in earlier years.

BORROWING

Some of the money the state spends is obtained through borrowing. The state constitution authorizes the issuance of short-term borrowing, in the form of tax and revenue anticipation notes. Until recently, the most important short-term borrowing occurred each spring before the state received the bulk of its income tax receipts. Each spring the state would borrow billions of dollars to advance local assistance funds to school districts and local governments; this became known as "the spring borrowing." However, the Omnibus Fiscal Reform Act of 1990 established the Local Government Assistance Corporation (LGAC) as the vehicle by which the state would end this annual cash flow borrowing. LGAC's mission is to sell up to $4.7 billion in bonds to allow the state to accelerate payments to local governments back into the previous fiscal year; this eliminates the huge "bump" in spending during the first quarter, as well as the need for cash flow borrowing to finance these payments. As of fiscal year end 1992-93, $3.3 billion in LGAC bonds had been issued, with the state's "spring borrowing" needs reduced commensurately.

To allow the state to obtain resources to finance capital construction, the constitution authorizes the issuance of bonds backed by the full faith and credit of the state treasury, known as general obligation debt. With two limited exceptions, these bonds may be issued only after approval by the voters. Such approval has been difficult to obtain. In the last 20 years, the state has received voter approval for general obligation debt only for transportation and environmental purposes.

Full faith and credit debt includes borrowing that has been approved by voter referendum, as well as borrowing that is directly authorized by the constitution (such as that for public housing or higher education). As of the end of the 1992-93 fiscal year, this outstanding debt was $5.4 billion.

Over the years, the state has developed a number of other ways to finance its capital construction programs. Using a mix of financing programs, public authorities may finance, construct, and/or operate a broad range of public benefit programs. These authorities perform essential government functions, such as building of housing, mental hygiene facilities, roads and bridges, mass transit facilities, prisons, and university facilities.

Public authorities, even those with local jurisdiction, are created by state law. Legally, they are public benefit corporations and are not subject to constitutional restrictions on the gift or loan of state money. For the same reasons, state and local debt limitations do not apply to them and they may incur debt without voter approval. The authorities are subject to public regulations and their boards of directors are appointed by elected government officials, such as the governor or a mayor.

Originally, the purpose of the authorities was to construct revenue-producing facilities of a public benefit nature and to operate them on a self-sustaining basis (through fees paid by those who use the facilities). The legislature has expanded the role of authorities to provide long-term financing for New York City and to operate mass transportation systems that require operating and capital subsidies.

In some cases, the state, subject to voter approval, guarantees bonds issued by an authority. State credit secures bonds issued by the Job Development Authority, the New York State Thruway Authority and the Port Authority of New York and New Jersey. On March 31, 1993, $478 million of such debt was outstanding.

Another state involvement with authority finances was moral obligation financing. The statutes creating the moral obligation debt programs of authorities established a procedure for the state to meet deficiencies that might arise in a corporation's debt service reserve fund. The deficiency would be the result of a failure of the project being financed to meet its mortgage payments. Since the fiscal crisis of 1975, authorities (with the exception of the Municipal Assistance

Corporation for the City of New York (MAC)) have been limited as to the maximum amount of moral obligation debt they may issue (MAC was limited in 1984). The amount of such debt outstanding as of March 31, 1993 was $7.9 billion, almost two-thirds of which represented MAC debt.

A major form of borrowing is called lease-purchase, which has financed various types of state facilities, including higher education projects, mental health facilities, and prisons. In these financings, bonds were issued by a public authority or a local governmental unit. Debt service on the bonds is paid with monies received from the state. Title to the facility is held by the bond issuer, with the state receiving title after bonds are fully retired. As of March 31, 1993, $10.6 billion of lease-purchase bonds were outstanding, the vast majority of which were issued by public authorities.

The state also utilizes the issuance of contractual-obligation debt by the public authorities to advance state programs, such as housing and mass transportation. Under this type of financing, a public authority issues debt that is supported by payments from the state. The debt issuer, however, does not generally receive title to the facility being financed. A total of $8.2 billion of contractual-obligation debt was outstanding on March 31, 1993, all issued by public authorities.

In addition, in 1985 equipment purchases for state departments and agencies began to be financed through obligations known as Certificates of Participation (COPs). This method of financing is less expensive than straight lease-purchase payments since it enables the state to access the lower interest rates prevalent in the short- to intermediate-term bond market. As of March 31, 1993, outstanding COPs totaled $592 million.

Clearly, any financing for which the state is responsible for making debt service payments must be taken into account in any evaluation of the state's fiscal operations or status. Some of the largest state public authorities are the Dormitory Authority, Medical Care Facilities Finance Agency, the Urban Development Corporation, the Metropolitan Transportation Authority, the Port Authority of New York, and the New York State Power Authority.

PART TWO

LOCAL GOVERNMENT

Local governments existed on the American continent before state and national governments were established and their structure and powers served as models for the larger bodies. Today, under our federal system, the state is the political unit with constitutional and statutory provisions that determine the powers and the very existence of all local governments within its borders. Indeed, local governmental units are commonly called "creatures of the state," and the state supports and regulates their activities. Everyone who lives in the state is a resident of one of New York's 62 counties, a city or town, and a school district. With the exception of the five counties known as boroughs in the city of New York, the territory of each county is wholly divided into cities and towns. Twenty-one counties have towns only.

A town may have one or more villages within its borders. Villages may lie in more than one town, or even in more than one county, but a village may not lie within a city.

Counties, cities, towns, and villages are called general-purpose local governments because each provides a number of services. Since counties and towns were originally formed to serve as administrative arms of the state, they are known as involuntary subdivisions or units of government. Villages and cities, on the other hand, were formed at the request of their residents and are considered voluntary jurisdictions.

Local governments have been in existence in New York for over 300 years. In that time, they have evolved into a many-layered system that serves as the point of delivery for many national and state governmental programs. The sharing of responsibility with other levels of government emanates from the state constitution. State laws grant power and authority to local governments. For local governments to carry out such responsibility, however, requires adequate authority and fiscal resources. It is apparent in many cases that their ability to raise money has not kept pace with the growth of their responsibility.

In future years local governments are likely to face ever greater challenges and stresses. Continuing revision of constitutional provisions and state laws affecting local government will undoubtedly provide for future changes in local government organization, power, and capability to administer and finance public services.

7.
MUNICIPAL GOVERNMENTS: COUNTIES, CITIES, TOWNS, VILLAGES*

There is no standard population or land size for the four types of municipal governments in New York State. The entire state is divided into counties, which are further divided into towns and cities. Many towns also have one or more villages within their borders. The sizes and shapes of municipalities are based on historical factors rather than a logical overall plan. A few municipalities were in existence before New York was a state. For example, the cities of Albany and New York had charters granted by the king of England in 1686 that gave them the legal right to conduct business as municipal corporations. The New York colonial assembly, which made important decisions before the American Revolution, was made up of representatives from each county. Since 1777 when New York became a state, the number of municipalities has grown. Today there are 62 counties, 932 towns, 62 cities, and 556 villages. Indian reservation lands have a separate legal status.

FOUR TYPES OF MUNICIPAL GOVERNMENTS

Counties

Originally county governments were formed to build courthouses and jails, poorhouses, and orphanages. These public buildings re-

*By Marjorie Shea, with acknowledgment to the New York State Constitution and the briefing book, compiled by the Temporary State Commission on Constitutional Revision (1994), and especially the chapter, "Intergovernmental Relations," by Richard Briffault.

quired taxpayer support and management. The supervisors of the various towns within a county would meet to make decisions about their financing and administration. This was the origin of the county board of supervisors which still serves as the legislative body in some counties. In the 1960s, the United States Supreme Court interpreted the Equal Protection clause of the Fourteenth Amendment to the U.S. Constitution to require "one-person/one-vote." Before that time, each town in a county, small or large, had one vote in the legislative body; i.e., a voter in a town with a population of 100 had 10 times more clout in the county legislative body than did a voter in a town of 1,000. Counties were ordered to correct this. Some counties kept the board of supervisors arrangement but gave the vote of each town representative a different weight. Other counties ignored town lines and drew districts of roughly equal population. The 57 counties outside New York City have legislatures, mostly called the County Legislatures.

Another major change in county government in recent years has been the establishment of a separate executive branch to administer the county. In some cases a county executive is appointed by the legislature and is responsible to that body. In many urban counties, however, voters elect a county executive. This type of executive has a power base independent of the legislature. All counties elect a district attorney and most elect a sheriff; both offices are described in the New York State Constitution. Other optional elected officials are treasurer, coroner or medical officer, and clerk.

Cities

New York State's cities vary greatly in size, from tiny Sherrill in Oneida County, with a population of 2,864, to giant Buffalo, the second largest city in the state, with over 328,100 people. New York City is in a class by itself. While three of the smallest cities have a commission form of government, where the legislative body is made up of department heads individually elected by the people, most cities have either a mayor-council form of government or a council-manager plan.

Mayor-council cities have an elected mayor, who heads the exe-

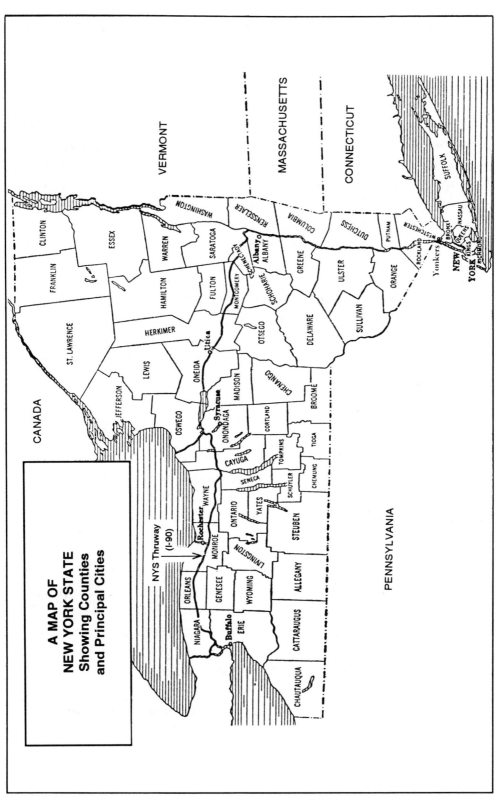

A MAP OF
NEW YORK STATE
Showing Counties
and Principal Cities

Figure 7-1

cutive branch, and a city council made up of representatives from wards or districts, forming the legislative branch. Cities with a mayor-council form of government vary widely as to the amount of power given to the mayor. Some cities have a strong mayor who may veto council proposals, appoint and remove agency heads, and present a budget. A strong mayor acts as a check on the council. At the other extreme, a weak mayor is merely a ceremonial figure, and standing committees of the city council run the agencies and prepare the budgets. In reality, most cities have a blend of strong and weak mayoral forms of government. Usually, the personalities of the mayor, the leader of the city council, and other elected officials will determine which form will be predominant.

The council-manager form of city government has an appointed professional manager hired to administer the city. The council is the policy-making body, and the mayor is mainly a ceremonial figure. The manager usually has the power to appoint and remove department heads and to prepare a budget, but does not have veto power over council actions.

Towns

People generally think of cities as being larger than towns or villages, but this is not so. In the last few decades as people have moved to the suburbs, many towns and villages have gained in population. For example, the Town of Hempstead on Long Island has twice the population of the City of Buffalo.

The number of towns within a county varies from 32 in rural Cattaraugus County to three in urban Nassau County. About half the towns in the state are in rural areas with populations under 2,500. Towns that have experienced suburban population growth provide many of the same services as a city. In many places, the town hall functions like city hall. The legislative body is usually the town council, with members elected at large, and a town supervisor to perform administrative duties. Town citizens elect two town justices to serve in their town courts. (Nassau and Suffolk counties, however, have District Courts rather than Town Courts.)

Villages

Historically, villages were formed when a group of people in one area of a town wanted a specific service, such as police and fire protection or street lights. Under state law they were allowed to form a corporation and to be taxed for a service that the rest of the town did not need. The legislative body of a village is the board of trustees, typically composed of four members plus a mayor. Since the 1980s, many larger villages have created the office of village manager or administrator. State law gives villages the power to make zoning ordinances that allow village residents to personalize their community. For example, the village board may decide to declare a special district for historic preservation or maintain a "greenbelt" or village square.

Land use planning is a major function of modern towns. This is also true in cities and villages. These municipalities are encouraged by the state to draw up comprehensive plans for construction and development of land within their boundaries. Based on this plan, the locality makes zoning laws, describing the types of construction or economic activity that can be done on a certain piece of property. Zoning laws may regulate everything from logging to the height of the buildings. They may restrict property owners from certain uncontrolled use of their property, such as building too close to a property line or turning a home into a hotel. They may also control site designation and construction of certain projects, such as where in a neighborhood a landfill will be constructed. Because residents have concerns for their neighborhoods and often become upset when zoning and land use changes are proposed, public hearings are required so that residents can voice their opinions. After taxes, land use decisions are the most hotly discussed public topics in local communities today.

NEW YORK CITY

Chartered as "Greater New York" in 1898, New York City consists of five counties (boroughs): Bronx, Kings (Brooklyn), New York (Manhattan), Queens, and Richmond (Staten Island). Forty percent of the people who live in New York State live within New York City. It is the largest city in the United States with 7.3 million residents counted in the 1990 federal census.

When the state legislature writes general municipal laws for other cities and counties within the state, it often provides a special category for "cities over a million" or "cities not within a county"—this means New York City. It is one of a kind.

The 1990 New York City Charter sets the basic rules of city government. The charter gives specific powers to designated officials and states how far those powers can be extended. As the city's chief executive, the mayor has the power to appoint agency and department heads, propose a budget, veto council bills, and negotiate agreements with labor unions. Also, the mayor's office must approve large purchases and leases. Some departments, such as police, fire, and sanitation, provide services typical of other cities in the state but on a much larger scale. Other departments, such as health, social services, and environment, administer county services and act as a division of the state departments.

New York is the only major city in the country with a municipal hospital system. It consists of 16 municipal hospitals and a number of community health centers. Also unusual in terms of size is the New York City Housing Authority, which operates over 300 projects that house over 500,000 people.

New York City's 1994 budget was $31.2 billion. This is more than was budgeted for 48 of the 50 states. One-third of the budget comes from state and federal aid and is earmarked for specific programs. The mayor is responsible for preparing an expense budget for day-to-day operating costs and a capital budget for construction and physical improvements. The City Council must approve the budgets.

Legislative powers are given to the City Council, which is made up of one representative from each of the 51 districts. Each district has a population of about 140,000. The council elects one of its members to be its leader. This person is called the speaker. The speaker is in charge of the daily operations of the council and hires staff, sets the agenda and time of meetings, and assigns members to committees. As the city's single lawmaking body, the council has the power to make major decisions on budget and spending priorities. It also has the power to make land use decisions, including zoning changes, housing, and urban renewal plans. Such plans require action by the city Planning Commission and often result in extensive public hearings.

When legislation is being considered by the council, it is called an "Introduction," often abbreviated to "Intro." or "Int.," and is assigned a number. When an Introduction is signed by the mayor it becomes a Local Law and is assigned a new number. The council also passes Home Rule Messages asking the state legislature to pass laws to benefit the city.

The charter has a system of checks and balances. The mayor proposes the budgets, appoints leaders to run city agencies, and approves or vetoes bills. The City Council votes on the budgets, gives consent on many important appointments to boards and commissions, and may override the mayor's veto by a two-thirds vote. The council, working through committees, holds regular oversight hearings of city agencies to determine how well their programs are working.

Every four years, beginning in 1993, voters of the city elect a council member and a mayor. In addition, two other city officials are elected—the comptroller and the public advocate. The comptroller has the power to audit the books of city agencies and to ensure that programs are running efficiently. New York City is the largest issuer of municipal bonds in the nation, and the comptroller, along with the mayor, arranges for their sale. Independently elected, the comptroller is given the power to act as a check on the mayor. The public advocate acts as an ombudsman, votes in the council in the rare case of a tie, and acts as the mayor in an emergency.

The five borough presidents are also elected every four years. With duties that are partly ceremonial and partly administrative, they represent the interests and special concerns of their boroughs at city hall. They have professional staffs who prepare environmental impact

statements for building projects and planners who encourage economic development. In cooperation with the heads of city agencies,
they oversee key services, such as street cleaning and garbage collection, and maintenance of public buildings and parks.

The city is divided into 59 community districts. Each district has
an unsalaried community board. Up to 50 members are appointed to
each board by the borough president, half of them on the nomination
of the local council members. These boards hold public hearings and
provide a forum where people discuss neighborhood concerns. The
boards make recommendations on public buildings, such as shelters
for the homeless and such private developments as "Trump City."
The volunteers who serve on these boards hire a manager and staff
to operate the district office.

LOCAL GOVERNMENTS: POWERS AND RESTRICTIONS

The United States Constitution, the basic law of the land, gives a
great deal of power to each state but says nothing about the powers
of local governments. The New York State Constitution governs what
a municipality can and cannot do. The two main provisions are Article IX, the "Home Rule" article, and Article VIII, the regulations for
local finances.

Home Rule Powers

Article IX establishes the home rule principle of local popular control of local government. It gives counties, cities, towns, and villages
the power to:

- adopt and amend local laws
- have a legislative body elected by the people
- appoint or elect other local offices
- take, by eminent domain, private property within municipal
  boundaries for public use
- make agreements with other governments to cooperate on
  projects

Regulations on Local Finances

Home rule principles do not apply to local finances. Article VIII applies to school districts, as well as to counties, cities, towns, and villages, and places restrictions on spending, borrowing, and taxing. Among its provisions are the following:

- limits the amount and type of borrowing
- limits the amount of real property taxes that may be raised
- prohibits loans of public money or property to any private undertaking

Examples of State Restrictions and Constitutional Limits

The state's role in municipal financing was dramatically underscored in 1975 when New York City was threatened with bankruptcy. The city was unable to raise money for its capital needs or sell its notes and bond to investors. The state created a Municipal Assistance Corporation (MAC) that for 10 years sold bonds for the city, backed by the state's credit.

Because this action linked the state's financial welfare to that of the city, the legislature also created the Financial Control Board (FCB) to exercise controls and supervise the city's fiscal planning. The FCB consists of the governor, the mayor, the state and city comptrollers, and three citizens appointed by the governor, with the advice and consent of the state Senate.

Another example of the state's role, although on a much smaller scale, occurred in the city of Yonkers. In 1988 Yonkers was paying large fines imposed by the United States District Court for failure to comply with a court-ordered housing desegregation plan. To support the financial well-being of Yonkers, the state imposed a citywide hiring freeze.

Other constitutional limits on local officers include:

- state legislature may provide for vacancies and for removing officers for misconduct

- terms, powers, and duties of certain county officers, including sheriff, county clerk, and district attorney, set by the constitution
- most government workers appointed by the Civil Service Merit System, with pension and retirements systems guided by state rules
- local court system and education system must follow uniform state rules
- localities that provide low-rent housing and nursing homes must follow state rules

Home Rule Requests

The New York State Legislature can pass general laws relating to local property or government if those laws apply equally to all counties, all cities, all towns, or all villages. If the state legislature wants to pass a special law that applies to one or more, but not all, it may do so only if there is a request by two-thirds of the members of a local legislative body. This is called a "home rule request." A special law may also be enacted by a message of necessity from the governor, who must factually demonstrate that an emergency exists; it must receive a two-thirds vote in each house.

Local-State Conflicts

Conflicts may arise when it is not clear if a certain activity should be managed by the state or by the local government. While the state has the responsibility to protect all of the people within its borders regardless of where they live, local governments may claim that their home rule rights are denied. When conflicts cannot be worked out politically, the two sides turn to the courts. In recent years, most rulings by the Court of Appeals, the state's highest court, have been in favor of the state.

SPENDING BY LOCAL GOVERNMENTS

Local government expenditures may be divided into capital out-

lay, debt service costs, and current operating expenses. Capital out-
lay covers such construction projects as schools, bridges, and sewage
treatment plants. Debt service is the payment of principal and interest on borrowed money. All other local costs fall into the current operating expense category.

Statistics show that local governments in New York State spend
most of their money in three major categories—education, social services, and public safety. Total spending by local governments within
all 50 states has increased dramatically; in New York it doubled between 1980 and 1990. During that decade, a national recession increased the need for the public to provide food, clothing, shelter, and
health care for needy individuals and families. Most programs administered by localities in these categories are mandated by the U.S.
Congress and the state legislature, leaving local legislative bodies
little discretion or choice in the size and scope of these programs.

For example, Medicaid is an $8 billion national program, giving
medical care to needy individuals no matter where they live in the
United States. County social services offices provide for the actual
medical treatment and preventive care. New York State receives
money from the federal government for approved expenditures; in
return the state pays the county for a portion of its costs. The state
Department of Social Services oversees local governments to ensure
that programs are carried out correctly. Funds may be withheld from
any county that does not follow the rules and regulations.

Mandated activities are programs that require a local government
to assume a specific responsibility or follow a certain policy. Some
examples of mandated activities are:

- The state requires that local treasurers keep financial records
  using a certain accounting system or a specific computer program.
- Municipalities must file yearly reports with the state
  comptroller's office to assure continued state and federal aid.
- In the 1970s and 1980s, the state relocated mental patients from

state institutions. Local officials dealt with this as it affected
their communities.

• The federal Americans with Disabilities Act of 1990 required
that local transportation systems provide access to the disabled.

These actions often have an impact on local budgets, and it is
difficult to project the costs.

Funding often accompanies mandated activities; but more and
more, local governments complain that state or federal government
monies do not cover the costs. Because municipalities are begging
for "mandate relief," legislative proposals now have a *fiscal impact
statement* attached to them. This means that the United States Congress and the New York State Legislature must consider the cost to a
locality before imposing any new or revised programs on them.

INCOME TO LOCAL GOVERNMENTS

Property Tax

The largest part of income to a local government comes from the
property tax. This is the tax that is "closest to home." When local
governments plan their budgets, they must project how much is to
be spent or appropriated and then deduct expected income from other
sources, such as state and federal aid and estimated sales and personal income taxes. At this point, the difference between expenditures and income is filled by the property tax; it is used to balance the
budget. Increasing public protest has forced localities to look for other
sources of revenue, as home and business owners threaten to vote
out of office any politician who approves an increase in property tax
rates.

Sales Tax

In the early 1990s, 13 of New York State's 62 counties increased
the sales tax in their locale. This is a tax on consumer goods and is
collected at the cash register and shared with the state. Although re-
tail businesses complain about the loss of shoppers to neighboring

communities, a sales tax of one-half cent receives less notice than several hundred dollars in a property owner's annual property tax bill. For this reason, government officials in cities and counties find it easier to increase the sales tax rather than the property tax.

State and Federal Aid

Individuals pay taxes to the federal and state governments, which return some of this money to local governments. State aid has accounted for approximately one-quarter of local revenues in recent years. Federal aid, however, as a percent of revenue gradually declined in the late 1980s and early 1990s.

The state and federal governments usually designate, in broad categories, the purpose and manner in which their aid monies may be spent. In the 1990s, federal aid fell into four main categories: education, environment, health, and human services. (Examples include maternal and child care, social services, Aid to Families with Dependent Children (AFDC), food stamps, justice (drug control and juvenile justice), and job training for the homeless.) At one time, the bulk of federal aid to states and localities was given for building capital improvements, such as highways, bridges, airports, and sewers. Now, a larger share of the federal funds goes to aid individuals in the areas of education and job training. Social services also receives a larger share of federal funds.

Other Taxes and Fees

Some cities in New York State collect revenue from a city income tax. Other revenue sources for municipalities are taxes on public utilities, hotel rooms, and commercial rentals. People are charged for building permits and fishing licenses. Governmental bodies also receive income from fines for parking and traffic violations.

Some types of taxation not only provide revenue but are meant to change people's behavior. For example, a per unit fee for the use of municipal water may encourage conservation. Towns and villages find that the total amount of trash is reduced when people have to pay a per bag fee for trash disposal. Limited parking spaces are rationed when coins must be put into parking meters.

EVOLVING RELATIONSHIPS

Since the 1960s, the federal government has made laws and interpreted the constitution in ways that affect local governments in every state in the nation. The "one-person/one-vote principle" of the United States Constitution has forced changes in representative bodies. Also, all state and local governments must conform to federal civil rights laws, particularly the Voting Rights Act of 1965 as amended, which states that all elections (federal, state, and local) must not discriminate in any way against minority groups. The federal courts will decide discrimination charges in these cases.

Today, suburban towns and villages face many of the problems traditionally associated with densely populated urban areas. Crime and air pollution do not stop at the city line. People look to all four types of municipal governments for good roads, clean water, and a healthy business climate. As different levels of local government seek similar powers to deal with problems and deliver services, the distinctions between city, village, and town forms of government become much less.

ASSESSMENT AND EQUALIZATION

Assessment

The taxing and borrowing powers of local governments and school districts, as well as the payment of various types of state aid, are based on the value of their real property. Each city, town, and most villages independently establish the assessed value of property. The Real Property Tax Law requires all assessments to be at full value. Historically, however, real property in New York State has usually been assessed at a percentage of full value. Inequities have long existed among and within different classes of property.

In the 1970s, these inequities stimulated a series of court challenges to the property tax assessment system of the state. Prompted by severe judicial criticism of assessment administration, the New York State Board of Equalization and Assessment prepared detailed analyses of assessment reform. Legislation was passed to set a time frame for assessing real property at full value. State financial assistance for reassessment was approved. A temporary state commission was set up to study the impact of implementing the full value assessment standard. The time frame for implementation of full value assessment was extended several times by the legislature, with reassessment still not occurring in a great many communities.

The temporary commission, in its report of 1979, recommended that assessment of property continue to be at full value. Recognizing that doing this would likely shift a substantial burden of the real property tax to residential property owners, the commission recommended consideration of a series of tax policy alternatives in order to soften the potential shift in burden.

Contrary to these recommendations, in 1981 the legislature repealed the full value assessment required by the Real Property Tax Law. This legislation authorized fractional assessment based on a uniform percentage of the full value of each parcel of property. In addition, except in New York City and Nassau County where a classification system is used, cities, towns, and villages are authorized to reduce the tax burden on residential dwellings for three or fewer families relative to other types of property. Fractional assessments continue to differ from place to place and within the same community.

The state legislature had mandated training for local assessors and, in some of the larger communities, the establishment of complex assessment offices. However, the percentage of communities basing their assessments on a percentage of full value is estimated at less than 7 percent. To add to the problem, property inflation and deflation in some communities has further eroded confidence in the equality of the assessing system. Court relief from overassessment (certiorari) and assessment at full value of newly sold property (the "welcome stranger policy") are among the reasons many are demanding change. In the ideal community, all properties of equal value (what a willing buyer would pay to a willing seller) should have the same assessment. In 1992 the state Board of Equalization and Assessment launched a program in which the board performs assessments within some localities that are extremely out of line with no semblance of equality.

Equalization

Because school districts overlap municipal lines and fractional assessments differ for each community, the state establishes and applies an equalization rate designed to make assessments among different local governments comparable in terms of full value.

The equalization rate is the percentage of full value by which the state Board of Equalization and Assessment judges the locality to assess its property. In this process, local assessment rolls are checked, data studied, and local assessors consulted to determine the levels of assessment and changes made since the previous year. (The greater the inequity or the lower the assessment rate, the more the equalization rate exacerbates the differences.)

A local government's equalization rate also determines the amount it can borrow. For example, a village's debt limit is based on 7 percent of its average full valuation (assessed value divided by the equalization rate) over a five-year period. Therefore, a lower equalization rate results in an increased full value computation and, consequently, a higher debt limit. (A municipality's value is merely the adding of all the assessed properties within the municipal limits.)

The need to raise the quality of local property tax systems and administration has resulted in efforts at both the state and local levels. Some municipalities have taken corrective action to remove assessment inequities. Better assessor training has been provided, and all assessors must be trained, whether elected or appointed. Records have been improved, and new tax maps have been made (all parcels of property now have tax map numbers).

Even with all this, there is still a great deal of work to be done. The lack of understanding of how the system works has been the biggest drawback to equality. Many property owners mistakenly believe that if their assessments rise their taxes will also rise. This explains the lack of political will to correct the tax rolls. All monies to be raised by a municipality are determined by the budget, then the amount is divided by the assessed value of the community. The closer to full value each parcel is assessed, the fairer the system is to all.

8.
LOCAL DISTRICTS AND AUTHORITIES*

No examination of how local government operates would be complete without a description of districts and authorities. Local districts and authorities have one thing in common—each district and each authority exists to provide a single service. Districts fall into three categories: school districts, fire districts, and special improvement districts.

SCHOOL DISTRICTS

Just as the entire area of the state is divided into counties, and the counties into towns, cities, and villages, the entire area of the state is divided into school districts. The boundaries of these districts do not necessarily follow town, city, village, or even county boundaries, except in the case of the larger cities. School districts are described in Chapter 9.

FIRE DISTRICTS AND FIRE PROTECTION DISTRICTS

Under New York State Law, fire districts have the legal status of "district corporations" that may contract debt and require the municipalities within which they exist to levy taxes on their behalf. They are independent units of local government.

Cities and villages may have fire departments to protect their residents. Towns, however, have no authority to provide fire protection

*Special appreciation to Janet Allen for her assistance.

as a town service, although they may create the position of fire marshal to inspect schools, hospitals, and other institutions and to grant permits for the storage of gasoline and chemicals.

Historically, population in towns was sparse, and fires were more a personal than a communal threat. Early fire protection came from neighbors forming bucket brigades. Following the bucket brigade came a loosely knit group with some firefighting equipment. From this beginning sprang the modern-day volunteer fire companies.

For many years, volunteer fire companies supplied fire protection without governmental assistance or support. Gradually, however, expanding town populations, the high cost of equipment, and the need to provide the volunteers with compensation in case of duty-related death or injury forced the independent fire services to look to government for help. In towns this was solved, not on a townwide basis, but through the establishment of districts on an area-by-area basis. These districts took two differing forms: fire districts and fire protection districts.

Fire Districts

Like school districts, fire districts may have boundaries that cross town and even county lines. Residents of the fire districts in the state elect the governing bodies, five-member boards of fire commissioners. One commissioner is elected each year to a five-year term, with elections held in December. The boards of fire commissioners operate under Section 176 of New York State Town Law.

A fire district is empowered by the state to determine its own budget, and the town (or towns) in which it lies has no authority to change a fire district budget. The district depends on the parent town(s) only for its creation and the collection of taxes to meet its needs. Fire districts have neither constitutional tax nor debt limits, but have strict statutory limitations on their finance authority. In many cities and villages, fire districts are created by municipal governments, which also control their budgets.

The single purpose of a fire district's board of commissioners is to make provision for fire fighting within the district. To do so, the commissioners often establish their own fire department or company to do the actual fire fighting. In other cases, particularly in rural areas, the commissioners of a fire district may contract with a neighboring village or fire district for service rather than setting up their own department.

Fire Protection Districts

Fire protection districts, on the other hand, are quite different from fire districts; they are not separate from town government. They have been set up by town governments for the purpose of providing fire protection by contract, usually with a nearby village or a neighboring fire district, for fire fighting services. The town board serves as the governing body of a fire protection district, as it does for a water district or a street lighting district.

IMPROVEMENT DISTRICTS

When part of a county or town requires a service not otherwise provided, that county or town may create a special district within which the service may be administered and financed. Units of local government may join together to serve some of the residents of each and charge back to those residents each unit's share of the cost. Among the services provided in this way are water, sewage disposal, refuse and garbage disposal, snow removal, sidewalks, public parking, parks, libraries, and public docks.

The creation of any new special districts with independent boards has been forbidden since 1932. Only a few, mostly on Long Island, are still administered by independent boards of commissioners rather than by town officials.

County Improvement Districts

A county improvement district may be created under New York

State County Law to provide water, sewer, drainage, or refuse disposal service to part of a county. These districts are used increasingly in the state to broaden a service area beyond the boundaries of a single municipality without covering the entire county. Charges for the service provided are paid by those who receive the benefits, without imposing financial obligations upon taxpayers outside the area served.

Town Improvement Districts

When part of a town requires a service not otherwise provided, the town may create a special district under New York State Town Law to administer and finance the service. These districts are not considered local governments because they do not exist independently of the towns that form them. Their budgets are approved by the town board, with members serving as commissioners of the district.

The largest number of districts provide drainage, fire protection, street lighting, sanitary sewers, and water. Other services that can be provided by improvement districts include ambulance, street curbing, garbage collection, health services, and public parking.

Revenues for many special improvement districts come from property taxes, although some districts are financed by either a unit charge or a formula based on acreage, front footage, water use, or some other factor.

PUBLIC AUTHORITIES

The public authority is another mechanism by which a specific service may be provided. Authorities are classified as public benefit corporations. Each is created for a specific purpose, such as the provision of water, sewage service, housing, or parking facilities. They are established by action of the state legislature.

Authorities commonly are established within a city or a county to provide a service, such as housing. Regional authorities providing transportation services (roads, bridges, tunnels) often encompass several counties. Chapter 6 discusses how these authorities are financed from sources outside of the state budget.

PART THREE

SERVICES TO STATE RESIDENTS

The people of New York State receive a broad range of services from the state government. Of these, the state's role in education, welfare, health, mental health, and environmental protection deserve particular attention since, in one way or another, they affect the lives of most citizens. These services account for more than 70 percent of the state's total expenditures, and their quality and cost is a matter of intense public interest.

Responsibility for providing these services is now shared by state and local governments. The dual basis of finance and supervision is intended to keep important functions of government close to the people while insuring uniform, minimum standards of service across the state. However, expanding concepts of the obligations of government to its citizens have encouraged huge expenditures by localities as well as by the state.

Local governments have protested vigorously the fiscal burdens of state-mandated standards and programs and have pressured the state, with its broader revenue base, to assume a growing share of the costs.

At the same time, localities have tried to retain a voice in policies governing the delivery of services. Tension and conflict over responsibility for providing these services and for funding them are likely to mold state-local relationships for some time to come.

9.
EDUCATION IN NEW YORK STATE*

Education has been a basic responsibility of government throughout our nation's history. Free public education has been a cornerstone of our democracy, and New York has taken justifiable pride in
its educational system and the achievements of its students. New
York's second largest public expenditure is for education (after social services); the average per-pupil expenditure in the elementary
and secondary schools is among the highest in the nation. New York
operates the nation's largest single system of post-secondary education. (California has more than one system.)

During the 1980s, the state increased its share of funding the cost
of elementary and secondary school education. By the end of the
decade, however, increasing demand for social, health, and prison
services, coinciding with decreasing state revenues, shifted costs back
to the local districts.

By 1994 education in New York appeared to be at a crossroads.
Revenues from the state and local sources were barely able to finance
the programs needed by a growing student population. At the same
time, citizens were questioning the effectiveness of American education.

*By Evelyn M. Stock, with special acknowledgment to Janet Walker of Westchester-
Putnam School Boards Association; Pat Keegan of the State Education Depart-
ment; Kenneth Goldfarb, State University of New York; Rita Roden, City Univer-
sity of New York; Terri Standish Kuon, Commission on Independent College and
Universities; Helene Hanson and Dr. Gil Jacobson, Southern Westchester BOCES;
Diane Remmers, New York State School Boards Association; and Suzanne Spear,
State Education Department.

DID YOU KNOW . . . that New York is one of five states to
have received the most immigrants during the 1980s?

The student body and the population in New York had changed.
There were more children, partly as a result of a record number of
immigrants during the previous decade. Many of these immigrants
did not speak English and needed additional services. Changing
family lifestyles created new needs. There were more divorces, more
single parent families, more homelessness. Most women now worked
outside the home and were not at home when children were dis-
missed from school. Social and medical problems affecting the schools
included more teenage pregnancies, dropouts, violence, drug and
alcohol use, and child abuse, as well as a new need for AIDS education and prevention.

NEW PROGRAMS FOR CHANGING NEEDS

Schools hired additional social workers and psychologists, insti-
tuted or expanded courses in bilingual education and English for
Speakers of Other Languages (ESOL), provided meals and after-school
programs for both students and their families, and offered comprehensive health services. Debate occurred in many districts as to exactly what services should be provided. The state mandated new
bilingual education programs and requirements, and recommended
development in 1992 of a new multicultural curriculum emphasiz-
ing contributions made by non-European cultures.

New York State also felt the effects of nationwide criticism of education that had begun in the 1980s. Schools were blamed for failing
to provide their graduates with the skills needed to function successfully in a global economy. In spite of the huge growth in education
funding and the achievement of some students, tests showed that
many American students lagged behind their European and Asian
counterparts. One solution proposed a free market approach to education—choice—which would enable parents to use public funds in
the form of vouchers or tax credits to pay for private education. Others warned this would destroy the public school system. Some districts provided choice within the public school system by creating

magnet schools (schools that specialize in a theme, such as computer education, arts, or sciences, with parents then given a choice as to which school their children will attend). New groups formed questioning the relevance of public education.

Some steps the state has taken include:

New Compact for Learning, a plan that seeks to focus more on student/learner outcomes, demands more involvement by parents and teachers—the stakeholders in a child's education—and allows for more local control.

Workforce Preparation Program, a pilot program to provide students with an improved transition from schools to the workplace. This program further promotes the business-school partnerships and internship programs that now exist.

Special Commission on Educational Structures, Policies and Practices, appointed in 1993, under the auspices of the Moreland Act. Its report made many recommendations and underscored the fragments of educational policy in New York State. What long-term effects the report will have are yet to be determined. Several earlier commissions have examined the New York educational establishment and made recommendations, but no action was taken.

FINANCING EDUCATION

DID YOU KNOW . . . that the major source of funding for education is from local property taxes and that the amount of state aid a school district receives depends on the wealth of the district?

School districts are separate units of local government with independent power to tax and to spend public money, except in the largest cities where education costs are paid out of general city funds. Property taxes are the major source of funding for most local school districts. Districts vary in the amount of property wealth and income behind each student. Some districts possess large industrial and business wealth; others rely solely on taxes paid by homeowners.

While there are broad state standards and state aid is used to subsidize less affluent districts, the programs offered, class sizes, and the condition of the physical surroundings in each district have traditionally reflected its residents' character, needs, and willingness and ability to support education. The result is a great difference from district to district in school tax rates and in the amount spent per pupil. Public revenues also fund health services, textbooks, transportation, and certain other programs offered in nonpublic schools.

The federal government provides approximately 3 percent of support for education in New York State. These funds have been targeted mainly in the following areas:

- science, foreign languages, and mathematics
- services to provide assistance to school districts for the education of low-income families, including preschool education, enrichment, language instruction for non-English speaking students, clothing, meals, health services, guidance, and remedial reading
- school library resources, textbooks, and other instructional materials
- teacher training and curriculum development

All school districts in New York State receive financial assistance from the state, ranging from 5 to almost 80 percent of their budgets (in all, the state pays approximately 40 percent of the money spent on elementary and secondary education). The money is budgeted each year from the General Fund, the proceeds of income, and business sales taxes; a very small amount comes from the lottery. State aid is allocated to school districts using a formula established by the legislature. The share each district receives has been determined by the number of students (weighted by special needs and grade level) and the local real property wealth, income, and tax effort behind each pupil attending its public schools. The goal is to ensure a basic level of financial support for all children in the state. In addition, the legislators try to respond to special needs of New York City and rural areas.

The state aid formula and the amount to be given in state aid are subjects hotly debated when the state budget is considered each year. Districts join together to protect the formula that assures their aid; others point to new problems that need increased funding. Affluent school districts argue that all districts are entitled to some return on the tax dollars they send to Albany. Legislators try to balance the needs of the districts they represent with the proposals for aid submitted by the Board of Regents, the governor, other legislators, the New York State School Boards Association, and the Educational Conference Board—a consortium comprised of school teachers' unions, superintendents, business officials, administrators, Parent-Teacher Associations, and the Public Education Association, among other organizations.

New financial costs were created by the need to repair and replace aging facilities after years of neglect and to remove lead paint and pipes. Federal and state mandates requiring districts to remove asbestos also consumed vast amounts of education dollars.

At the same time, many districts found that their assessment rolls were declining, most for the first time. Real estate tax certiorari proceedings* eroded tax bases significantly. Homeowners in record numbers also challenged their assessments. Higher taxes for the remaining taxpayers were then needed to repay the businesses and to compensate for the declining assessments.

Thus, when the state drastically cut state aid in 1990, local districts were forced to discontinue programs, reduce staffs, increase class sizes, and postpone maintenance. Innovative methods were initiated to share services with other districts and municipalities. Consolidation and merger possibilities were explored. Some local districts established foundations to provide a new source of funding. At the same time, local property taxes rose in response to the decline in revenues.

---

* Court challenges to reduce the assessed valuation of property, which, if successful, will not only reduce future taxes but also may award repayments for taxes previously paid.

The final ingredient to this mixture was a change in the voting population. For some time, citizens without children had been the majority in most districts. Now with so many immigrant families unable to vote, this group had unprecedented political power. Even those who wished to support education were caught between fixed incomes and increasing local taxes. Citizen groups banded together demanding cuts in education spending. Although state aid was increased in 1993, the spring of that year saw a record number of budget defeats. Anti-tax groups ran candidates for school boards, insisting that New York education make do with less. Taxpayers and legislators called for other methods to finance education. New executive and legislative proposals demanded more reliance on the income tax to finance education.

The question of exactly what determines equity and fairness in education, and how much financial support the state should provide to achieve it, has been debated in New York and in the nation since the 1970s. In some other states, the question has been, and continues to be, decided by the courts. Another question is what role the state has in supporting excellence.

STRUCTURE OF EDUCATION IN NEW YORK STATE

The task of education is one of the unspecified powers reserved to the states by the 10th Amendment of the United States Constitution: "The powers not delegated to the United States by the Constitution, nor prohibited by it to the State, are reserved to the States respectively or to the people."

The New York State Constitution empowers the legislature to "provide for the maintenance and support of a system of free common schools, wherein all the children of the state may be educated" and grants legal authority to the State Education Department and school boards to carry out educational duties. The various statutes governing education are contained in New York State Education Law, a separate body of laws. The legislature delegates authority to the Board of Regents and the State Education Department. In turn the state delegates powers to school districts which are considered branches or agencies of the state government.

DID YOU KNOW . . . that the University of the State of New York (not SUNY) is over 200 years old and is the umbrella agency for all educational institutions in New York State?

University of the State of New York

Established by the state legislature in 1784, the University of the State of New York is the oldest state educational agency in the United States. All approved educational institutions in the state come under its umbrella. Directed by the Board of Regents, the university's purpose is to govern and regulate all educational institutions in New York State. These include all public and private elementary and secondary schools in the state; all privately and publicly controlled institutions of higher education—also covering the schools in the State University of New York (SUNY) system; and all libraries, museums, and other educational and cultural institutions admitted to or incorporated by the University (see Figure 9-1).

New York State Board of Regents

The governing body of the University of the State of New York, the Board of Regents, was also established by the state legislature in 1784. Sixteen regents serve on the board, one from each judicial district and four from the state at large. Each is elected by the state legislature for a five-year term. (Until recently the terms were 15 years.) Each serves without compensation. The board elects its own chairman or chancellor and meets monthly.

The regents possess broad authority to charter, register, and inspect educational institutions; establish and stimulate education extension work; and conduct exams, confer degrees, and grant credentials. They supervise requirements for admission to a broad range of vocations and to all professions, with the exception of law. They set licensing standards for both business and professions. They define the needs and goals of education to the governor, to the legislature, and to the people of the state. They select the President of the Uni-

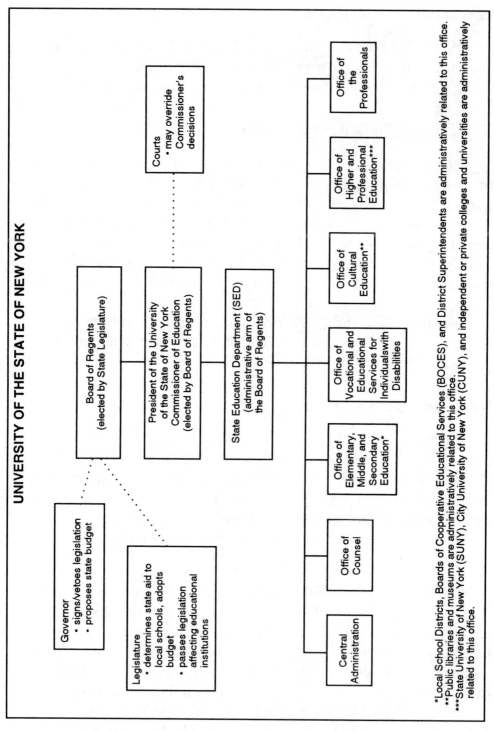

UNIVERSITY OF THE STATE OF NEW YORK

Governor
• signs/vetoes legislation
• proposes state budget

Legislature
• determines state aid to local schools, adopts budget
• passes legislation affecting educational institutions

Board of Regents
(elected by State Legislature)

President of the University of the State of New York
Commissioner of Education
(elected by Board of Regents)

State Education Department (SED)
(administrative arm of the Board of Regents)

Courts
• may override Commissioner's decisions

Central Administration

Office of Counsel

Office of Elementary, Middle, and Secondary Education*

Office of Vocational and Educational Services for Individuals with Disabilities

Office of Cultural Education**

Office of Higher and Professional Education***

Office of the Professionals

*Local School Districts, Boards of Cooperative Educational Services (BOCES), and District Superintendents are administratively related to this office.
**Public libraries and museums are administratively related to this office.
***State University of New York (SUNY), City University of New York (CUNY), and independent or private colleges and universities are administratively related to this office.

Figure 9-1

versity of the State of New York who also is the Commissioner of Education and who serves at the pleasure of the regents.

President of the University of the State of New York/ Commissioner of Education

The president serves as the chief executive officer of the State Education Department. Powers and duties include enforcing educational laws, executing all educational policies set by the regents, supervising all schools and institutions covered by education law, granting and annulling teaching certificates, reviewing appeals and petitions, and executing all duties determined by the regents. The commissioner sets and enforces the Commissioner's Regulations, a body of rules that govern the operation of the institutions under his/her control. The commissioner has quasi-judicial as well as executive power, which includes power to hear appeals in matters involving the educational community and questions on codes or rules adopted in an individual school district. Rulings are subject to judicial review.

State Education Department (SED)

The administrative arm of the New York State Board of Regents, under the direction of the commissioner, SED is responsible for administering the state's educational policies. It also provides teachers and school administrators with advisory services on curricula and all areas of school management, plus higher education, cultural education, professional responsibility, and vocational and educational services for individuals with disabilities.

TYPES OF SCHOOL DISTRICTS IN NEW YORK STATE

DID YOU KNOW . . . that there were once 11,000 separate local school districts in New York?

All elementary and secondary schools are organized into school districts. In 1994 there were 715 local school districts, ranging from small elementary school districts of less than 100 students to New York City with over one million students, from affluence to poverty,

SCHOOL ADMINISTRATION ON THE LOCAL LEVEL:
MAJOR TYPES OF SCHOOL DISTRICTS IN NEW YORK STATE

	COMMON SCHOOL DISTRICTS	UNION FREE SCHOOL DISTRICTS	CENTRAL SCHOOL DISTRICTS (ALSO CONSOLIDATED)	CITY SCHOOL DISTRICTS and ENLARGED CITY SCHOOL DISTRICTS	
				Population over 125,000	Population under 125,000
DEFINITION	Limited to operation of elementary schools. Of 19 such districts in 1994, 13 operated schools. The balance contracted with other districts.	Authorized to operate junior and senior high schools as well as elementary schools. 153 in 1994 and 16 Special Act Districts.	Formed by combining existing districts to provide better facilities and larger areas for taxation and administration. 467 in 1994.	Buffalo, New York City, Rochester, Syracuse, and Yonkers.	Wholly or partly within a city of less than 125,000. May combine with adjoining Union Free or Common School Districts to pool resources of the larger area. 57 in 1994.
BOARD OF EDUCATION				N.Y.C.: Governed by special statutory provision for 32 semiautonomous elected local boards and a central board responsible for high school and other designated functions. Others: 3 to 9 members, four- to six-year terms. Buffalo, Rochester, and Syracuse elect boards. Yonkers and New York City have mayoral appointees.	
Size	1 or 3 trustees	3 to 9 trustees	5,7, or 9 trustees		5, 7, or 9 members
Term	Three-year terms	Three- or five-year terms	Three- or five-year terms		Five-year terms
How Selected	Elected	Elected	Elected		Elected; in one city, however, they are appointed by the mayor.
ADMINISTRATION	Superintendent appointed by the Board of Education, by contract; serves at pleasure of the board.				
BUDGET	Must be voted on each year by voters. Boards unable to achieve approval of the budget at district elections are authorized to operate schools under austerity programs. Decision may be made at an annual meeting held on any Tuesday between May 1 and June 30. If school district divided into election districts and voting machines used, a district need only schedule a public hearing to discuss expenditures. The hearing must be scheduled not more than 30 nor less than 10 days before budget vote is to take place.			Part of a total city budget adopted by the City Council	Adopted by board after a hearing.
ELECTIONS	At Annual Meeting or on day designated for public vote (see above), usually in the spring. Nominations by petition with minimum of 25 signatures. Absentee voting for school board members only, at local option, in districts having personal registration.			New York City Central School Board and Yonkers have appointed boards. Elections are scheduled in May or June, except Rochester and Syracuse where vote is in November.	1st Tuesday in May, general and special registration. Nominations by petition with minimum of 100 signatures.
TRANSPORTATION	Required for all public, private, or parochial school students: K-6, living 2 to 15 miles from school; those in grades 9-12, 3 to 15 miles. Changes may be made at option of local board, but state aid is paid only for 2 to 15 miles. Districts must provide door-to-door transportation for handicapped students, ages 5-21, within 50-mile radius. Districts receive 90% state reimbursement for transportation costs incurred the previous year.				Optional at discretion of school board to any grade level, or all. If provided, must include equivalent service to public, private, and parochial students. Mileage requirements same as for preceding districts.

Figure 9-2

from high density areas to rural isolation.

The major types of school districts in New York State are common school districts, union free school districts, central school districts, and city school districts. They differ in educational and transportation services provided, budgets (voting and finance), and elections of school board members (see Figure 9-2).

Common school districts were first created by the state legislature in 1812 to operate elementary schools (kindergarten through eighth grade). They are also responsible now for ensuring that their resident children receive a secondary education.

Union free school districts were authorized in 1853 to operate high school programs, although some do not do so. "Special act" school districts, grouped under union free districts, are religious or charitable institutions authorized by the state legislature to receive state financial aid.

Central school districts, formed by combining common, union free, and other central school districts, may operate high schools.

City school districts are of four types, the boundary lines of which are the same as that of a city. These include those with populations under 125,000; enlarged city school districts; central city school districts; and five with populations over 125,000 (known as the "Big Five"—Buffalo, New York City, Rochester, Syracuse, and Yonkers). The budgets for the Big Five are part of a total city budget adopted by the city councils of each. Citizens of city school districts do not vote for their budgets.

In addition, three "central high school" districts provide only secondary education to children from two or more common or union free school districts.

RELATIONSHIP BETWEEN LOCAL SCHOOL BOARDS AND THE STATE

School districts are governed by elected boards of education (Yonkers and New York City have appointed boards) who have the authority and duty to adopt policies, to select the superintendent, and to present a budget to district voters (except in cities). School boards oversee and manage a public school district's affairs, personnel, and properties as outlined in New York State Education Law. Boards usually serve as advisors to the superintendent on many issues beyond their legal responsibility.

School board members are local officers; however, they must carry out functions mandated by the state constitution, state legislature, and State Education Department. Legislative action affects employment policies for teachers, governs school election procedures, and defines the jurisdiction of boards of education in other ways.

In New York City, the board of education is a quasi-independent agency established by the state legislature. It is responsible for the city's public elementary, junior high school, and high school system. The board consists of seven members, two appointed by the mayor and one by each borough president. It is responsible for determining education policy for the one million children in the New York City public school system. The board employs a chancellor to administer the system.

In 1969 the state legislature created community school districts (now 32) in New York City. Each community school district has a nine-member elected community school board which administers the elementary, intermediate, and junior high schools in the district. The school board members, who serve for three years without salary, are residents of the district or parents of children in the schools. These boards hire community superintendents and principals, set budget priorities, and make budget recommendations to the central board. They have some curriculum and program discretion but the final education authorities in the city are the chancellor and the central board of education.

BOCES

Boards of Cooperative Educational Services (BOCES) are regional, voluntary, cooperative associations of school districts established by an act of the New York State Legislature in 1948. They share planning, services, and programs to provide educational support activities more economically and efficiently than can be provided by individual districts. In 1994 39 BOCES in New York served from seven to 56 local districts. Most school districts in New York State belong to a regional BOCES; membership is not available to the Big Five cities.

Originally focused primarily on vocational education and special education, BOCES' broad array of services now include special education programs for students with many different disabilities, occupational education for secondary school students and adults, advanced placement, and advanced-level courses for gifted or talented students. Adult education includes upgrading and retraining programs, high school equivalency preparation, English for Speakers of Other Languages, and workplace literacy. BOCES also offers staff and professional development programs for teachers and administrators, management and instructional technology support services, student transportation services, transportation safety training, field trip services, and school bus maintenance services.

Each BOCES is governed by a board comprised of five to 15 members serving three-year terms. They are elected by the boards of education of the member school districts. The geographical area covered by a BOCES is known as a supervisory district; districts range in size from 183 to 3,312 square miles. The chief administrative officer is a district superintendent.

The district superintendent also performs duties assigned by the Commissioner of Education, serving as the State Education Department's field representative in the supervisory district. A BOCES appointment of a district superintendent is subject to the approval of the Commissioner of Education.

STATE UNIVERSITY OF NEW YORK (SUNY) SYSTEM

The State University of New York (SUNY) is one of the components of the University of the State of New York. Before its creation in 1948, there were 32 state-funded public colleges acting independently of one another. Following the upsurge in college enrollment after World War II, New York created the SUNY system with coordinated statewide goals and policies and an expanded mission that included the establishment of research university campuses. Soon after, the state embarked on a massive construction program for SUNY to meet the growing higher education needs of the state. Today, it is the nation's largest and most comprehensive single system of higher education. Its campuses now include: four university centers, including two medical schools, two schools of dentistry and a law school; two health science centers; 13 colleges of arts and science; four specialized colleges; six two-year agricultural and technical colleges; five statutory colleges on two independent university campuses; and 30 locally sponsored community colleges.

In the fall of 1992, SUNY's state-operated schools and community colleges had more than 25,400 full- and part-time instructors and an enrollment of more than 40,000 credit students at 64 campuses.

CITY UNIVERSITY OF NEW YORK (CUNY) SYSTEM

The City University of New York (CUNY), another component of the University of the State of New York, traces its beginnings to the Free Academy founded in 1847, the forerunner of the City College and Hunter College, which was founded in 1870. The state legislature established a municipal college system in New York City in 1926. As demand for higher education grew, other colleges were established within the city's system. In 1961 the state legislature designated the municipal system as the City University of New York (CUNY), mandating that CUNY expand to meet the increasing demands for postsecondary education. In response to the city's fiscal crisis in the mid-1970s, the state legislature increased state financial support and mandated the university's educational mission.

CUNY, the nation's leading urban university and third largest university system in the country, comprises nine senior colleges, seven community colleges, one technical college, a graduate school, a law school, a medical school, and an affiliated school of medicine. In 1993 CUNY had about 6,000 full-time teaching faculty at more than 70 research centers and institutes. Approximately 207,000 students were enrolled in degree courses, and another 150,000 in adult and continuing education courses at campuses throughout the five boroughs of New York City.

INDEPENDENT COLLEGES AND UNIVERSITIES

New York is home to more independent colleges and universities than any state in the nation. Independent higher education began here in 1784 when New York State seized control of King's College from the British and renamed it Columbia College. (Columbia College is now part of Columbia University in New York City.) Until World War II, independent colleges and universities were the state's major providers of higher education.

Today, New York's independent sector includes 136 research universities, liberal arts colleges, technical institutes, and specialized schools with more than 150 campuses. Fifty-six campuses are located in New York City. Thirty-nine are on Long Island and in the other immediate suburbs of New York City. Thirty-seven are in upstate urban areas, including Buffalo, Rochester, Syracuse, Utica, Albany, and Poughkeepsie. The remaining 19 independent sector institutions are scattered throughout the state's rural regions. Collectively, New York's independent colleges and universities are the state's largest private employer with more than 100,000 employees. In 1992-1993 the independent sector enrolled more than 273,000 undergraduate and 128,000 graduate students in full- and part-time programs.

THE FUTURE OF EDUCATION

The remainder of the 1990s promises more discussion about the role of the state in education, the governance and funding education will receive, and how to define the proper balance between equity, excellence, and fairness.

They key questions will be:

- How much will New Yorkers be willing to pay for education?
- Who will pay—the state or local districts?
- What type of tax should support education—property, income, or sales?
- What services should be provided by the schools?

As the debate continues, it will be interesting to see if New York State schools will be able to respond to the many challenges they face.

10.
SOCIAL AND HUMAN SERVICES*

The care of those in need has been a public responsibility in our country for three centuries. Our concept of this responsibility has expanded gradually over the years to include children in many categories of need and others who have become dependent through unemployment, accidents, old age, illness, blindness or other disability, or through the death of the family breadwinner. The goal of the New York State Department of Social Services is to ensure that dependent or disabled persons receive financial and medical assistance or other supportive services necessary to achieve the greatest degree of independence possible.

The Department of Social Services has basic responsibility not only for income assistance programs but for day care and all aspects of child welfare, including neglected and abused children, adoption, and foster care. Protective services are provided for persons 18 or over, who have physical or mental impairments that prevent them from providing for their most basic needs, or who are unable to protect themselves from neglect or abuse if they have no one responsible, willing, or able to help them. These services may include living arrangements in an adult family home or assigning a person to handle money management tasks. Other adult services include senior centers, programs for displaced homemakers or abused wives, and family planning counseling.

The department is headed by a commissioner appointed by the

*By Barbara Gibbs.

governor, with the advice and consent of the Senate. The department is organized into eight program divisions and four support offices that have primary responsibility for administration, establishing programs, setting policies and regulations, and implementing state and federal mandates.

Locally, social services are administered through 58 social service districts found in every county and in New York City. These social service districts are headed by local commissioners, who operate local programs and administer state programs under directives and standards of the New York State Department of Social Services.

Public assistance falls into two major categories: delivery of services and delivery of money. The former includes help for families, children, and individuals, and is not limited to those who receive cash assistance. It may come from agencies other than the state Department of Social Services. Housing relocation, counseling, mental hygiene, day care, employment training, and supportive services to the elderly are examples of such services.

Programs that carry cash benefits are generally designated as income maintenance. They include Aid to Families with Dependent Children (AFDC); Home Relief (HR); and Supplemental Security Income (SSI) for the aged, blind, and disabled. In addition, the medical assistance program (Medicaid) provides cash payment to those providing medical services and nursing home care for the needy; the Food Stamp Program provides cash assistance in the form of nonnegotiable food purchase coupons; and the Home Energy Assistance Program (HEAP) provides cash assistance to help offset the home heating costs of eligible households.

A complex web of intergovernmental financing supports these programs, and the mix may be different for each program. This complicates their administration, but each program can be understood if looked at in the light of who administers and delivers the cash payments, who is the source of the money, and who is responsible for identifying those eligible to receive it.

The federal government pays 50 percent of the cost of Medicaid and AFDC, with the state and localities sharing equally in the remainder. Home Relief is funded half by the state and half by local governments. Food stamps and SSI are fully funded at the federal level, although New York adds a state supplement to the SSI payment. In New York State, all income maintenance programs are administered through the Department of Social Services, except SSI which comes under the jurisdiction of the Social Security Administration. The number of programs and the amounts expended for them, however, do not measure the level of assistance to the recipient. This is determined by two factors: the standard of need and the schedule of allowance to meet that need. As a general rule, the administrative agencies (either the U.S. Department of Health and Human Services or the state's Department of Social Services) define the level of need. It is up to the appropriate legislative body, either Congress or the New York State Legislature, to determine how much of the need will be met.

In 1990 the Department of Social Services disbursed over $24 billion. The largest portion, approximately $11.62 billion, was for medical assistance, which included Medicaid payments to hospitals, skilled nursing facilities, clinics, out-patient care, and home health and personal care. About two-thirds of Medicaid spending paid for services for the elderly and disabled. The income maintenance programs, AFDC and HR, were over $3.29 billion. Family and Children Services—child preventive/protective care, foster care, adoption, and day care—cost $1.74 billion. Other spending was spread among adult services, food stamps, SSI, HEAP, and local administration. Largely because of the economic recession, the number of people receiving public assistance is growing. In 1993-94 New York State spent about $1.9 billion on 2.1 million needy adults and children through AFDC, HR, and SSI. The state expects record-high caseloads in the near future.

During the 1980s, the federal government withdrew support from many social benefit programs. As a result, New York State has attempted to increase its commitment to those in need. In recent years special emphasis has been placed on the homeless, disabled needy adults, and children. A number of pilot programs have been established to assist pregnant teenagers. Emphasis has also been placed on preparing clients, including mothers of very young children, to support themselves and their families through training and employment programs. These programs often include transitional support services, such as transportation, health care benefits, and day care. The Department of Social Services has created a unit to supervise and regulate licensed day care, as well as to increase the supply of quality day care in New York State.

Beginning in 1993, AFDC Job Opportunities and Basic Skills (JOBS) programs are averaging 30,000 recipients a month. Day care for an estimated 74,000 low-income children, whose parents are working or receiving training, is state funded. Great strides are also being made securing parental support payments for dependent children; in 1992 collections increased to $460 million.

The Homeless Housing and Assistance Program (HHAP) was developed in 1983 and provides grants to support the capital cost of projects designed to expand and improve housing and shelter for the state's homeless population. Current efforts are aimed at finding alternatives to high-cost temporary shelters for families at risk of homelessness. Preventive services is working to move families more rapidly from shelters to permanent housing, and helping recipients pay rents that are in arrears.

HEALTH

The New York State Department of Health is responsible for safeguarding the health of New York's residents. To accomplish this effectively, the department is organized into two major program units: the Office of Public Health and the Office of Health Systems Management. The total budget for the department in 1992-93 was $1.26 billion.

The Office of Public Health (OPH) is responsible for preserving the health of New York State's residents through education, research, and prevention of accidents and diseases. Many of the programs administered by OPH are aimed at enhancing child growth and development through early prenatal care, newborn screening, supplemental foods for pregnant women and children, immunization, school health programs, and teen counseling. Other activities focus on occupational health hazards and the potential health threat of toxic contaminants in our environment. Still others are geared toward combatting communicable diseases through continued monitoring of drinking water purity and restaurant sanitation, and through follow-up investigation of hospital infections and sexually transmitted disease cases.

Research is also a major function of the Office of Public Health. Clinical, laboratory, and epidemiological studies are focused on such public health problems as birth defects, kidney disease, health manpower needs, toxic effects of chemical substances and radiation, sexually transmitted diseases, and cancer. Other research efforts aim to improve laboratory testing methods, expand our understanding of the body's basic biosystems, and reverse deterioration of our lakes and streams.

The Office of Public Health monitors the need for skilled health professionals throughout the state and identifies underserved areas for training support programs. It also oversees the medical conduct of physicians and takes disciplinary action against individuals who violate the law. Finally, OPH is responsible for maintaining records of every birth, death, marriage, and divorce that occurs in the state, and for protecting the confidentiality of those records.

The Office of Health Systems Management (OHSM) is responsible for assuring that quality medical care is available to all New York State residents regardless of where they live or their ability to pay. The Department of Health, through OHSM, has direct authority over all health care institutions in the state covered by the Public Health Law, including hospitals, nursing homes, diagnostic and treatment centers, and many home care providers. To protect the welfare of patients, the state certifies all health care institutions and sets standards governing nearly every aspect of health facility operation.

Ensuring that limited health care dollars are prudently spent and administering programs to keep the cost of health care services within affordable limits are other primary goals of OHSM. The Office of Health Systems Management develops reimbursement methods and sets the rate each health facility will be paid for services to patients covered by Medicaid. Those rates form the basis for Medicare, Blue Cross, Workers' Compensation, and no-fault insurance rates. OHSM also audits health facility costs and charges and reviews the financial implications of health facility construction and expansion. Finally, OHSM is responsible for statewide planning to assure that state health care resources are efficiently allocated.

The Department of Health operates specialized research and patient care institutions: Roswell Park Memorial Institute, a comprehensive cancer center in Buffalo; Helen Hayes Hospital in West Haverstraw, specializing in treatment of physical disabilities; and New York State Veterans' Homes in Oxford and on Long Island, both residential health care facilities for veterans and their dependents. These institutions also serve as statewide resources for the training of health professionals and dissemination of preventive health information to New York State residents.

New York leads the nation in its financial commitment to AIDS/ HIV education, prevention, and care. Breaking down barriers to quality primary and preventive medical care, focusing on health care issues critical to women, and responding to the escalation of rabies and tuberculosis are major concerns of the early 1990s.

MENTAL HYGIENE

There are three agencies responsible for mental hygiene: the Office of Mental Health; the Office of Mental Retardation and Developmental Disabilities; and the Division of Alcoholism and Substance Abuse Services.

During the late 1980s, New York State embraced community care as the cornerstone of its mental health system. Thousands of individuals were promised community-based care if they moved from state psychiatric facilities. Intensive case management by trained mental health professionals assists serious and persistently mentally ill individuals during crises and helps them find residential and treatment services. The community development program has opened 7,100 residential beds statewide and developed a system of day treatment, supportive employment, and vocational rehabilitation programs.

The average daily census at psychiatric centers in 1994 was about 10,000 due to the development of community residential and treatment program alternatives. The total state mental health appropriation for 1994 was $2.01 billion. New York State is continuing its multi-year effort to expand community-based residential services while maintaining, improving, and consolidating long-term psychiatric center inpatient buildings. Comprehensive Psychiatric Emergency programs are located at 10 sites statewide.

The Office of Mental Retardation and Developmental Disabilities (OMRDD) is mandated to assure the development of comprehensive plans, programs, and services in the areas of research, prevention, care, treatment, rehabilitation, and education and training of persons with mental retardation and developmental disabilities. Residential and rehabilitative services to educate or train the mentally or physically disabled are provided at 13 developmental centers and related special population units. By the end of 1993, 27,000 persons were living in community settings, including supportive apartments, supervised community residences, family care, and intermediate care facilities for the developmentally disabled.

As a matter of policy, placement of individuals into community residential settings from developmental centers is conditional upon the availability of appropriate day and support services. These services include education programs under the auspices of the New York State Department of Education; day-treatment programs accommodating substantially impaired individuals; day-training programs providing transitional training of individuals moving toward independence; and comprehensive vocational rehabilitation services, sheltered workshops, and supported work programs for those individuals capable of a greater degree of independent action. Supporting this system are networks of transportation, recreation, and social ser-vices. Altogether, 50,000 individuals can be expected to participate in day programs and more than 30,000 families will receive services to help them care for family members with disabilities.

Over 2.5 million persons in New York State have serious drug and alcohol problems; over 850,000 are addicted to drugs and 1.7 million adults and adolescents seriously abuse alcohol. When their families are included, over one-third of the entire population of the state is directly affected by the problem of alcohol and substance abuse. In 1992 the New York State Office of Alcoholism and Sub-stance Abuse (OASAS) was formed into a single state agency by the merger of the Division of Alcoholism and Alcohol Abuse and the Division of Substance Services.

Its "Mission Statement" is given below:

OASAS is responsible for identifying the personal, economic, and social consequences related to the consumption of alcohol and other drugs; designing, implementing, and advocating for policies and programs in prevention, early intervention, and treatment; and, in conjunction with local governments, providers, and communities, ensuring that a full range of appropriate and needed alcoholism and substance abuse services for addicted persons, family mem-bers, and others at risk are available and accessible in the commu-nity, providing a continuum of quality programming in a cost-effi-cient and effective manner.

Alcoholism services include inpatient facilities for detoxification, crisis, and short-term rehabilitation. Community residential facili-ties—recovery homes, halfway houses, and supported living resi-dences—comprise long-term programs. Eleven of the 13 state-oper-ated Alcoholism Treatment Centers are co-located on the grounds of the Office of Mental Health facilities. Detox, methadone maintenance to abstinence, and outpatient services are the major components of substance abuse programs. A special effort is targeted to chemically dependent youth in residential correctional facilities.

OASAS is the largest alcohol and drug treatment agency in the nation, treating more than 100,000 people daily. It has an annual budget of approximately $408 million.

LABOR

Of all the state's activities in providing services and regulating business and government, nowhere does it have a more pervasive impact than in the field of labor. There its policies affect almost everyone. In general, the state's labor activities, administered by the Department of Labor, fall into three categories:

- protection of wages, hours, and working conditions
- services to the unemployed, the underemployed, and the disabled
- the conduct of labor relations between employers and employees

The state Department of Labor is chiefly responsible for these functions. In addition, the Department of Civil Service serves as central personnel agency for state offices; and the Public Employee Relations Board (PERB) resolves disputes between state and local governments and their employee unions.

The Labor Department is headed by a Commissioner of Labor, who is appointed by and reports directly to the governor. Both the Civil Service department and PERB are headed by commissions, three members of which are appointed by the governor, with the consent of the Senate, for six-year terms. In each case, the governor is barred from naming more than two of the three from the same political party and is empowered to designate one of the three as chairperson.

Wages and Working Conditions

Perhaps the most encompassing labor standard in the state is that governing the minimum wage. The General Industry Minimum Wage Act, effective January 1, 1981, provides that all occupations (excepting farm workers) must be paid a minimum rate—$4.25 per hour in 1994. Farm labor is covered under separate protective wage policies of the state. General Industry Wage Orders, effective since January 1, 1987, permit specified allowances from the minimum wage for meals and lodging supplied by an employer. Employers are required to post Minimum Wage Information posters in their places of business.

These policies are administered by the department's Division of Labor Standards, which not only enforces minimum wages but strictly regulates hours of employment and working conditions for minors. The division also carries out inspections and investigates complaints relating to farm and home work establishments. A separate law provides for payment of the prevailing wage received by labor unionized workers on construction projects for any governmental agency.

The labor department is also responsible for supervising health and safety standards affecting the general public. The department administers the Public Employees Safety and Health Act and inspects places of public assembly, boilers, amusement parks, and ski tows. The federal Occupational Safety and Health Act (OSHA) provides enforcement of safety and health standards in private industry. State safety laws not covered by OSHA are enforced by the New York State Labor Department.

Workforce Services

New York State's employment services operate through a statewide local office network of the Department of Labor's Job Services. These act as placement agencies for skilled, unskilled, and professional job seekers.

The most widely used of the labor department's services is unemployment insurance, providing weekly benefits for up to six months (and longer in periods of high unemployment) to almost everyone, with the exception of domestic workers earning less than $500 a year, part-time student workers, farm workers, and the self-employed. Unemployment insurance payments are financed by an employer-paid payroll tax that varies according to a company's past employment and unemployment experience.

The state also administers the Workers' Compensation Law, providing cash benefits and costs of medical treatment (including rehabilitation) to eligible workers temporarily disabled because of work-related injury or disease. The dependents or the spouse of a worker who dies from such an injury or illness may also receive cash benefits. The amount of the benefit claim is determined by a panel of the Workers' Compensation Board, a body of 13 members appointed by the governor and confirmed by the Senate for seven-year terms.

In addition, the state requires most employers to carry coverage under its Disability Benefits Program that provides for cash payments to eligible employees who are temporarily disabled by illness or accidents that are not job related. In 1977 the legislature also authorized these cash payments as replacement for earnings lost because of pregnancy. Benefits under this program are paid by self-insured employers or their insurance carriers.

Through 69 Community Service Centers, the Department of Labor offers literacy education, job training, unemployment insurance, and job referral programs. The state participates in a number of training programs designed to increase the employability of workers. Some are on-the-job training funded almost entirely by the federal government. Among these are the Job Training Partnership Act (JTPA) in which the state acts as the administrator for local service delivery areas (SDAs). Job service programs and the Job Training Partnership Act make specialized training and placement services available to persons facing economic or educational barriers to employment. During 1991 federal JTPA adult training programs provided services to more than 38,000 individuals, with 14,000 placed in unsubsidized employment. State Department of Labor Job Service registered approximately 759,800 applicants for jobs and was able to place 80,500 individuals in jobs.

Job Training Partnership Act funds, available through the federal Economic Dislocation and Worker Adjustment Assistance Act, and the state Worker Adjustment Act help dislocated workers affected by plant closings or workforce reductions to return to the job market. During 1991, 18,000 individuals participated in the Dislocated Worker

Program, and almost 5,000 completed training. The Department of Labor also administers the Displaced Homemaker Program. The federal Summer Youth Employment Program and the state Youth Education, Employment and Training Program complement these efforts by providing economically disadvantaged youth with skills to promote retention and transition to employment services. Federal Urban Aid legislation, passed in 1992, provided an additional $46 million for the JTPA Summer Youth Program.

Since 1945, New York State has had a Division of Human Rights, the responsibilities of which include elimination and prevention of discrimination in employment as well as in housing and in places of public accommodation. Over the years, the statute defining the division's powers has often been amended to broaden its scope. Within the past decade, the division has focused on policies to promote minority participation in on-the-job training programs, employment in publicly subsidized construction, admission to labor unions, and, increasingly, to end practices that discriminate against women.

The division may generally adopt and promulgate rules and regulations, and investigate and pass on complaints alleging discrimination in employment in labor unions or in training programs on the basis of race, creed, color, national origin, or sex.

The work of the division has frequently been beset by complexities involving minorities, who demand larger quotas of jobs on publicly subsidized construction; contractors, who blame unions for inadequate numbers of qualified minority workers; unions, who blame contractors for inadequate on-the-job training opportunities; and the conflicting interests of the state, faced with timely completion of public works projects under conditions of fair employment.

The Division of Human Rights is headed by a commissioner appointed by the governor, with the consent of the Senate. Decisions of the division may be appealed to the New York State Human Rights Appeal Board. The board consists of four members appointed by the governor, with the consent of the Senate, for six-year terms.

Employer/Employee Relations

The state's Labor Relations Act governs relations between employers and their employees, guaranteeing workers the right to bargain collectively through representatives of their own choosing. The New York State Labor Relations Board administers this law and investigates complaints that rights of labor or management have been violated. The board is empowered to enforce the act through orders that may, for example, reinstate a discharged employee or mandate a company to bargain with an employee organization.

Like the labor relations board, the New York State Mediation Board consists of three members appointed by the governor, with the consent of the Senate, for six-year terms. Its function is to provide voluntary mediation services to the parties in a labor dispute. If the dispute affects the public interest and cannot be settled by mediation, the commissioner of labor may appoint a board of inquiry to hold public and private hearings, subpoena witnesses and take evidence, and to publish a report of its findings, thus bringing pressure to bear on the parties.

Labor relations for public employees are governed by the Taylor Law, enacted in 1967, to settle disputes between any state or local governmental agency and its employees. The law outlaws strikes and establishes a schedule of penalties that includes fines and jail sentences for violations. The Taylor Law outlines procedures for conducting contract negotiations, and the Public Employees Relations Board (PERB) mediates when the parties in a dispute are at an impasse. The most far-reaching effect of the Taylor Law is to establish the right of public employees to organize into unions and to bargain collectively.

In 1974 the Taylor Law was amended to require, for a trial period, binding arbitration in labor disputes between local governments and police and firefighters' unions. Since then, the legislature, at the urging of the unions, has extended the effect of the amendment. However, local government officials have argued that contracts financed through tax revenues should not be determined by arbitrators who are not responsible to the taxpayers.

HOUSING

The lack of affordable housing has been addressed for almost 70 years by the state government, beginning with the Housing Law of 1926 that established the New York State Board of Housing. The Division of Housing and Community Renewal (DHCR) has two major functions: it assists in the production and preservation of low- and moderate-income housing and it administers the rent-regulation system as it affects New York City. The DHCR was operated under the direction of the commissioner of the division, who was appointed by the governor and approved by the Senate. In 1985 the commissioner was appointed to the additional post of Director of Housing and became responsible for all housing activities in New York State, including the State of New York Mortgage Agency (SONYMA) and the New York State Housing Finance Agency (HFA). The state has acquired, constructed, rehabilitated, and preserved 225,000 affordable housing units in the past 10 years. Effective use of federal funds and tax credit incentives have encouraged production of another 47,000 units.

Home ownership is made possible by affordable mortgages and assistance with down payment and closing costs through the Affordable Home Ownership Development Program (AHODP) and the State of New York Mortgage Agency (SONYMA). Under a special program developed in 1992, SONYMA works with businesses to help their employees obtain home mortgages.

Other innovations in housing include the Low Income Housing Trust Fund Program, established in 1985, which administers the disbursement of $35 million to stimulate the development of affordable housing for low-income persons by rehabilitating or converting underutilized or vacant buildings. The Special Needs Housing Program improves the condition of single room occupancy (SRO) housing. Rural Rental Assistance provides rent subsidies to low-income families. Neighborhood and rural preservation programs, along with Rural Rental Assistance, are national models of public/private partnership. The Housing Finance Agency (HFA) provides low-cost financing to both not-for-profit and for-profit developers of rental housing who reserve 20 percent of the units for low-income tenants.

Home ownership is encouraged through the New York HOPE Program for Public Housing Tenants initiative. Housing Opportunities for the Elderly (HOPE), Public Housing Modernization, and Tenant Health and Safety provide funds to renovate existing housing and preserve its affordability.

After a 10-year absence, the federal government has joined with states to provide affordable housing assistance through the National Affordable Housing Act (NAHA), authorizing New York to award grants provided under the Federal Home Investment Partnership Program (HOME).

11.
ENVIRONMENT AND TRANSPORTATION*

ENVIRONMENTAL CONSERVATION

Stewardship of the lands and waters of New York State has been a state responsibility since the first state constitution, but the nature and extent of that responsibility have expanded enormously in recent years. Growing public concern for the environment led to constitutional changes, giving the legislature new authority to protect the state's natural resources.

In 1970 the Department of Environmental Conservation (DEC) was created, consolidating particular functions of the Department of Health and the Environmental Conservation Department (fish and wildlife) into a single agency mandated to protect and enhance our natural environment.

The department's major areas of responsibility were outlined: environmental quality and natural resources management. Environmental quality includes pollution control for air, water, and land plus hazardous and solid waste management. Natural resources management addresses protection and uses of our fish, wildlife, land, marine, and mineral resources. The DEC has continued to grow as the federal government, state legislature, and citizens become aware of unnecessary, alternative, and unacceptable methods of handling environmental issues.

*By Mildred Whalen.

Administration

A commissioner, appointed by the governor, directs the work of the DEC. The commissioner is charged with organizing and operating all divisions, regional offices, administrative offices, boards, and commissions. In addition, the commissioner represents the governor on regional commissions or at conferences formed by federal regulations or actions of individual state legislatures.

Central administration of the agency is conducted from its main office in Albany. There are nine regional offices that serve specific geographic areas of the state. These regional offices provide numerous services, including issuance of regulatory permits, technical and public education, assistance in the management of regional natural resources, and enforcement of environmental laws and regulations. Additionally, they are called upon by the commissioner to implement specific projects (see Figure 11-1).

Additional responsibilities of the DEC include serving on state planning commissions, overseeing hearings, law enforcement, legal affairs, and program and policy analysis (see Figure 11-1).

Office of Environmental Quality

Environmental quality encompasses a variety of functions with an underlying goal of limiting the amounts and types of pollution discharged into the air, water, or land. The office is divided into divisions responsible for air resources, solid waste (including hazardous or toxic substances), and water.

The DEC establishes standards to measure air, land, and water pollution. In conjunction with local and state health departments, it monitors and controls the release of polluting substances that may take the form of particulates, gases, dust, radiation, odors, liquids, nutrients, or thermal discharges.

DIVISION OF AIR RESOURCES
In 1957 New York State enacted one of the nation's first air pollu-

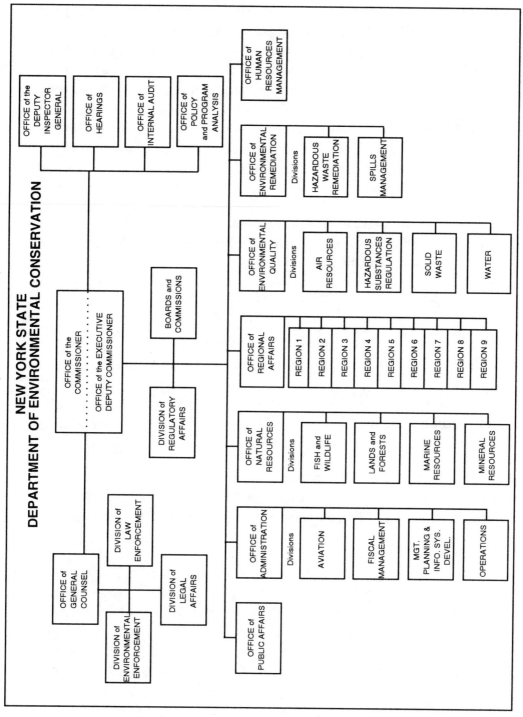

NEW YORK STATE DEPARTMENT OF ENVIRONMENTAL CONSERVATION

OFFICE of the DEPUTY INSPECTOR GENERAL

OFFICE of HEARINGS

OFFICE of INTERNAL AUDIT

OFFICE of POLICY and PROGRAM ANALYSIS

OFFICE of the COMMISSIONER

OFFICE of the EXECUTIVE DEPUTY COMMISSIONER

BOARDS and COMMISSIONS

DIVISION of REGULATORY AFFAIRS

OFFICE of GENERAL COUNSEL

DIVISION of LAW ENFORCEMENT

DIVISION of ENVIRONMENTAL ENFORCEMENT

DIVISION of LEGAL AFFAIRS

OFFICE of PUBLIC AFFAIRS

OFFICE of HUMAN RESOURCES MANAGEMENT

OFFICE of ENVIRONMENTAL REMEDIATION
Divisions
HAZARDOUS WASTE REMEDIATION
SPILLS MANAGEMENT

OFFICE of ENVIRONMENTAL QUALITY
Divisions
AIR RESOURCES
HAZARDOUS SUBSTANCES REGULATION
SOLID WASTE
WATER

OFFICE of REGIONAL AFFAIRS
REGION 1
REGION 2
REGION 3
REGION 4
REGION 5
REGION 6
REGION 7
REGION 8
REGION 9

OFFICE of NATURAL RESOURCES
Divisions
FISH and WILDLIFE
LANDS and FORESTS
MARINE RESOURCES
MINERAL RESOURCES

OFFICE of ADMINISTRATION
Divisions
AVIATION
FISCAL MANAGEMENT
MGT. PLANNING & INFO. SYS. DEVEL.
OPERATIONS

Figure 11-1

tion control laws. Since then New York, joined by the federal government in 1970, has operated a statewide air-monitoring network
that is periodically upgraded to detect new pollutants. In 1985 New
York became the first state to issue regulations to reduce sulfur emissions specifically in response to the acid rain problem. In 1993 the
state legislature passed the New York Clean Air Compliance Act
(NYCACA), which extends the control of the state over stationary,
nonpoint source air pollution (not coming from a smokestack), as
well as vehicle emissions, and establishes the Clean Air Fund to be
used for regulatory procedures.

Implementation of air pollution control programs has resulted in
some improvement to air quality around the state. However, the
state is required by the federal Clean Air Act to reduce pollution
approximately 15 percent a year starting in 1990 and continuing on
to the year 2007.

DIVISION OF SOLID WASTE
The Division of Solid Waste is responsible for regulating reduction, reuse, recycling, incineration, and landfilling of solid waste. It
also handles the clean-up of inactive toxic or hazardous waste areas
and regulates the handling of hazardous or toxic substances. (The
term solid waste refers to material formerly called garbage or trash.)

Permits are issued to operators of landfills, incinerators, and resource recovery facilities (incinerators that process waste for the purposes of converting it into a usable energy source). Permits are also
issued to users, handlers, and transporters of hazardous waste.

Reduction, while listed first in New York's solid waste hierarchy
of importance, has only been a voluntary effort. A recycling markets
office does exist on a very limited budget to inform and coordinate
the community-based solid waste plans. Each locality that develops
an incinerator or a landfill (called a disposal community) is required,
under the solid waste regulations, to develop a "Solid Waste Plan."
General Municipal Law requires all generators of solid waste material to separate certain categories of this waste, such as paper, card-
board, metals, and glass for recycling purposes. All generators, both

private and public, are required to "source separate." Statewide recycling began in 1982 with the Returnable Beverage Container Act, commonly called the bottle law.

Re-use has redirected materials that would have been sent for final disposal instead to purposes that employ them as usable resources. Incineration and resource recovery of solid wastes has not continued at the levels that existed in the 1980s. Many communities have experienced problems with the technology, and strong recycling programs have reduced the amounts of waste to be burned. Landfilling has proceeded with advanced processes that prevent leakage, promote compaction, and are flexible to meet community need.

The division has worked with local communities to locate, identify, and develop remediation plans for a wide variety of nonhazardous disposal sites. The 1986 Environmental Quality Bond Act (EQBA) was the source of funds for these purposes. A similar bond was defeated in 1990. In 1993, however, the state legislature passed the Environmental Trust Act to continue the remediation and other environmental purposes.

The Division of Solid Waste also handles control of hazardous substances, issues permits, and monitors the uses, handling, and transporting of identified hazardous substances. A "manifest system" tracks these materials from the generator to user, transporter, and finally the disposal facility. The system was developed to identify who is liable if a problem occurs at any point.

The DEC has developed an Inactive Hazardous Waste Site Remedial Plan that ranks sites based on their threat to the environment, induces responsible parties to fund cleanup sites, and uses state funds where responsible parties are unknown or unwilling to cooperate and where federal Superfund monies are not available.

DIVISION OF WATER

New York has approximately 70,000 miles of streams and 4,000 lakes. More than one-third of the state's population receives its drinking water from groundwater. It is the responsibility of the Division

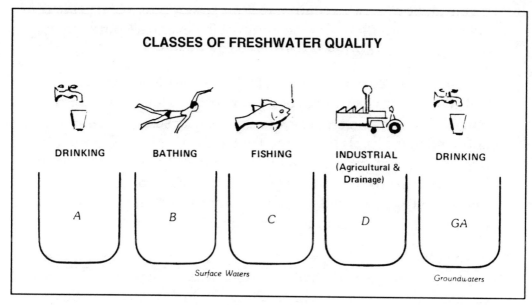

Figure 11-2

of Water to maintain high quality and adequate quantities of freshwater resources.

The division reviews the water quality classifications for all rivers, streams, and lakes. It has divided these classifications into five categories (see Figure 11-2).

Each water classification has its own set of water quality objectives and standards. Discharges into surface or groundwater must meet the standards for that particular water body. These discharges are regulated under the State Pollutant Discharge Elimination System (SPDES). This comprehensive water pollution control permit program specifies which substances and what amounts of these substances can be legally discharged into ground and surface waters.

Groundwater programs emphasize protection of aquifiers (underground geologic formations that store and transmit significant quantities of water) from contamination. Three specific projects assist with prevention of future contamination of underground waters:

1. the groundwater mapping project

2. the control programs for bulk storage of petroleum and hazardous substances

3. a spill response program for petroleum and hazardous substances

Chemical spills and leaks, along with nonpoint source pollution (usually agricultural, lawn, street, or highway runoff), are the principal current threats to our ground and surface waters.

Other water quality issues are managed in conjunction with the Division of Construction Management. These include such programs as wastewater facilities, flood control projects, and toxic and nutrient clean-up programs for lakes and rivers.

Focus on water quantity includes developing strategies for drought management and flow control. The goal of these programs is to ensure a sufficient water supply to support a wide range of usages across the state. The Division of Construction Management has developed a Water Resources Strategy Program to evaluate local water supplies and to recommend improvements. These recommendations may include advice on water conservation, metering, or other use/ management strategies. In addition, the division protects watershed areas from development that might endanger community reservoirs.

The federal Clean Water Act has had a significant impact on our state's waters. The federal government supplied uniform standards to deal with the problems of industrial contamination and local sewage treatment programs. The reduction of contamination has been in the public's best interests. Some riverine systems (rivers with all of their tributaries and streams) and lakes are significantly cleaner. Estuary programs are starting to show results; ending pollution discharges into our waters, while not totally successful, has slowed contamination. Citizen involvement in cleaning up our waters remains high, and officials recognize its importance.

The Coastal Zone Management Act deals with coastal waters, including ocean, sound, the Great Lakes, and the St. Lawrence River systems. The purpose of the act is to recognize sensitive environmental spaces where the land and the water interact, such as wetlands, estuaries, deltas, and riverine systems.

Office of Natural Resources

Natural resources management promotes and coordinates the state's waters, wetlands, forests and land, fish and wildlife, and marine and mineral resources. The Department of Environmental Conservation is mandated to assure their protection, enhancement, allocation, and balanced use for public benefit.

Resource management includes such activities as permitting wetlands to be used, issuing hunting and fishing licenses, stocking programs for support of species population or sport purposes, permitting conflicting uses (e.g., well-withdrawal permits on Long Island), protecting endangered and threatened species, permit oversight of gas and oil wells, protecting against forest fires, and directing search and rescue efforts by forest rangers along with local rescue teams.

DIVISION OF FISH AND WILDLIFE

The Division of Fish and Wildlife is organized in five major program areas: environmental protection, environmental management, species management, public use, and extension services. Activities of these programs include species inventories and monitoring, wildlife stocking programs, wildlife population management programs, and increased public access.

Environmental protection programs maintain productive habitats for fish and wildlife, in addition to protecting unique and essential environments. Some recent studies have focused on the impacts of acid deposition (acid rain), river sediments, and toxic contaminants on fish and wildlife.

One of the most popular programs in this division is the yearly rearing and stocking of more than one million pounds of trout, salmon, and freshwater gamefish in New York's lakes and streams. Optimum access and availability of fishing and other wildlife recreation has had a positive economic impact on the state's economy.

Extension services gain public support for wise management of fish and wildlife resources by making people aware of their value and availability. In 1982 the Return a Gift to Wildlife Program was established to fund a variety of education, conservation, and restoration projects (such as reintroducing the lynx) to improve New York's fish and wildlife resources and the public's enjoyment of them. Donations are made through a check-off procedure on the New York State Income Tax form. Over $20 billion has been contributed to the program since it was started.

DIVISION OF MARINE RESOURCES
The Marine Resources Division manages and monitors the conditions of New York State's marine crustaceans, finfish, shellfish, and seashore habitats. Tidal wetlands are identified for acquisition by state funds or bond issues, with the division managing these lands in cooperation with local governments to ensure appropriate public use and long-term preservation.

Biologists monitor marine populations of targeted species and develop procedures to protect and maintain them as a healthy resource. The division works with fishermen's organizations to protect the fishing economy in the state. Studies of the American lobster and certain shellfish are evaluating the impacts of commercial harvesting, tidal pollution, and tidal wetland development on species population levels.

DIVISION OF LANDS AND FORESTS
The Department of Environmental Conservation administers more than 3.7 million acres of land, including the Adirondack (over 2.5 million acres) and the Catskill (280,000 acres) forest preservation areas, plus more than 750,000 acres of state parks, reforested areas, and multi-purpose lands across the state.

Activities of the division encompass management and protection of state-owned lands; forestry programs, including harvesting and marketing of wood products outside the forest preserves and urban and rural education projects; and administration of the state pesticide program. Other key activities are the acquisition of sensitive or environmentally important lands and obtaining, where the public's interests are concerned, development rights or conservation easements.

Land acquisition programs have been funded by the Environmental Quality Bond Acts of 1972 and 1986. In 1993 the state legislature established the Environmental Trust Fund to acquire lands determined to be special by the New York State Open Space Plan.

Lands are purchased for a variety of reasons. Those lands identified by the Open Space Plan include areas that provide increased recreational opportunities and access for the general public, protect ecologically sensitive areas, consolidate existing state holdings, and preserve scenic views or areas.

The division also has a pesticide management program. The program trains and certifies farmers or commercial applicators. It also maintains a registry of pesticide businesses, registers all pesticides sold and used in the state, and enforces and administers all pesticide laws and regulations.

DIVISION OF MINERAL RESOURCES

New York ranks eleventh in the nation in the production of non-fuel minerals and leads the nation in the production of calcium chloride, garnet, and emery. Crushed stone, cement, zinc, sand, and gravel are also mined. In addition, there is extraction of such fossil fuels as oil and natural gas.

The Division of Mineral Resources controls the drilling and production of oil, natural gas, and solution salt, and regulates other types of mining to assure reclamation of mined lands. The regulatory program emphasizes protection of the land, water, and air through environmentally sound drilling practices, proper disposal of drilling fluids, restoration of mine and drilling sites, and proper plugging of exhausted and abandoned wells. A permit/inspection system is used to ensure compliance with the regulations.

Division of Regulatory Affairs

Two New York State laws are essential to the entire environmental regulatory process: the State Environmental Quality Review Act (SEQRA) and the Uniform Procedures Act.

The State Environmental Quality Review Act was developed to help the government and the public protect and improve the environment by requiring that environmental factors be considered along with social and economic considerations in siting buildings, uses, subdivisions, roads, and developments, and determining other uses and actions that are subject to the regulatory process. An environmental assessment form is required for all projects, with an Environmental Impact Statement (EIS) identifying significant negative effects on the environment for certain proposals. The EIS examines ways to reduce or avoid serious adverse negative impacts. The act (SEQRA) applies to any state or local government agency whenever it must approve or fund a private or public project. Project applicants are responsible for preparing the Environmental Impact Statement.

The Uniform Procedures Act complements the State Environmental Quality Review Act process by putting into the code of regulations a procedure for permit applications and a review process. The review process starts with the regional office staff and can conclude with a public hearing conducted by an Administrative Law judge.

Environmental analysts, located in all nine of the Department of Environmental Conservation's regional offices, review the permit applications. The status of projects and activities subject to DEC regulation is published weekly in the "Environmental Notice Bulletin."

The Division of Regulatory Affairs is also responsible for establishing criteria for the siting and design of a low-level radioactive waste disposal facility. This disposal facility was mandated by the federal government which requires state governments to handle low-level radioactive wastes from facilities, such as hospitals, laboratories, and nuclear power plants. Permit applications for temporary storage (on site) of low-level waste or permanent disposal of these wastes are also reviewed by this division.

Division of Law Enforcement

Enforcement of the Environmental Conservation laws, rules, and regulations is the role of environmental conservation officers and investigators. Their activities range from protection of endangered species to tracking illegal transport, storage, or disposal of hazardous wastes. Environmental enforcement personnel work closely with attorneys in DEC's regional offices, and other staff assist the division.

Watchdog of the Environment

Historically, New Yorkers have had a concern for the protection of the state's natural environment. Even before the state constitutional amendment in 1894 established the Adirondack Park as "forever wild," land use and water quality issues were being addressed on a regional basis. However, New Yorkers have abused other resources; for example, hazardous wastes in Love Canal, PCBs (polychlorinated biphenyls) in the Hudson River, and groundwater contamination on Long Island are a few that are more visible.

The natural environment and the Department of Environmental Conservation are not static. Dynamic forces, both natural and man-made, threaten the quality and quantity of our resources. As we enter the next century, the stewardship role of DEC will change. More information, discovered nearly weekly, is shaping its role as watchdog of the environment. It has to be accountable to the different forces that shape the state—the public, the business community, environmental groups, and state and federal law-making bodies—and test these against its own capabilities. The Department of Environmental Conservation will need to strike a balance between protection of our natural resources for future generations and pressure for growth and economic development.

TRANSPORTATION

History

A state department for transportation was the first agency formed by New York State. At the end of the Revolutionary War, the Office of Surveyor-General was established to survey lands vested in the state of New York. In 1817 the state engineer was charged with digging the Erie Canal, which was completed in eight years. A combined Office of State Engineer and Surveyor was established in 1946 and renamed the Department of Public Works.

The "good roads" movement began in New York as the state's privately owned dirt turnpikes became over 81,000 miles of paved public highways. The Department of Highways was established as a result of the Highway Act of 1909.

Prosperous times and the expansion of the suburbs following World War II resulted in unprecedented numbers of Americans purchasing automobiles, but public transportation did not keep pace. The ideal of individual mobility was now a reality as personal travel by auto more than quadrupled in the state.

This new mobility spurred expansion of commerce and an exodus of the newly affluent from the cities to the suburbs. A continuing cycle of more highways being built to accommodate increased traffic, traveling at greater speeds, has continued to this day. The parkways constructed in the 1920s and 1930s and the thruway system constructed in the 1950s became models for the national Interstate Highway System, mainly built during the 1960s and 1970s.

During the 1960s, while the Interstate Highway System was under construction, there was also an increasing demand for air travel and an expansion of Atlantic Ocean ports. To coordinate the development of each transportation mode, the Department of Transportation (DOT) was formed in 1960. The mandate of the department was to provide adequate, safe, balanced, and efficient transportation at reasonable cost to the people of New York.

**REGIONAL OFFICES
OF THE NEW YORK STATE DEPARTMENT OF TRANSPORTATION**

1 Albany
2 Utica
3 Syracuse
4 Rochester
5 Buffalo
6 Hornell

7 Watertown
8 Poughkeepisie
9 Binghamton
10 Hauppauge
11 New York City

Figure 11-3

Administration

Under the leadership of the commissioner of transportation who is appointed by the governor, the department's central office in Albany coordinates the work of the 11 regional offices throughout the state (see Figure 11-3). Each regional office is headed by a regional director who is responsible for services, construction, and maintenance programs within that region. These programs are coordinated with regional planning, county, city, town, and village programs.

The planning staff reviews all proposed projects to ensure that there is a balance between programs. Project plans and specifications are developed by a team of specialists: engineers, lab technicians, draftsmen, landscape architects, cartographers, photogrammatists, and computer analysts. Local public hearings are held for each project for public input and environmental review under the State Environmental Quality Review Act (SEQRA). Affected local governments are also asked for input before finalization of plans.

Project construction is performed by private contractors who bid competitively for each job. Department of Transportation (DOT) engineers monitor and inspect construction projects to ensure work is completed to contract specifications.

Highways and Bridges

The Division of Highway Maintenance is the largest in the Department of Transportation and is responsible for all of the state's highways and bridges.

The division provides assistance to local governments to help maintain over 100,000 miles of roads and over 11,000 bridges. Activities include pavement repair and marking, snow and ice removal, bridge repair, sign upkeep, shoulder and guardrail repair, roadside mowing, litter removal, drainage maintenance, and rest area maintenance.

Public Transportation

Each year there are over two billion bus, ferry, rail, and subway commuter passengers in New York State. Public authorities, local governments, private corporations, school districts, and non-profit agencies own and operate public transit facilities in the state.

The Department of Transportation's programs for capital assistance provide for purchasing buses and constructing new terminals and maintenance facilities. The department is responsible for regulating safety, service, and fare aspects of private intrastate public transportation operations, and conducts safety inspections of school buses and privately owned vehicles that provide public services.

The Public Transportation Safety Board investigates public transit accidents involving commuter rail, subways, buses, and their physical facilities.

New York's rail network consists of two major east-west lines, and one major north-south line with connecting branchlines and shortlines. Partnerships among the state, rail owners, private industries, and local governments have revitalized the railroads. Improvements by Amtrak and the DOT have produced a growing passenger rail system connecting communities across the state, as well as major connections with the national and Canadian systems.

Aviation

Every few seconds, an airplane takes off or lands somewhere in the state. Over half of these air passenger miles are for business purposes. The Department of Transportation provides financial aid, technical assistance and planning services, and assists with the operation of over 500 public and private airports.

Waterways and Ports

New York's major waterways—the Hudson River, the Great Lakes, the St. Lawrence Seaway, and the New York State Canal System—provide waterlinks throughout the state.

The ports of New York City, Albany, Buffalo, Oswego, and Ogdensburg play a vital role in both national and international trade. The number of recreational boaters has increased tremendously during the last quarter century, while there has been a decline in commercial water traffic. To accommodate all of these various interests, the Department of Transportation provides planning and technical assistance, along with state loans and grants to port authorities for equipment or facility construction and rehabilitation.

Financing Improvements

In the 1960s and early 1970s, highway expansion received the emphasis with little attention given to the upkeep of existing roads. The financial recession of the mid-70s forced New York State to cut back on many state programs, including bridge and highway maintenance. While the 1973 oil crisis resulted in drivers purchasing fuel-efficient automobiles, the number of miles driven continued to increase, resulting in wear and tear on the highway network. Yet fewer fuel tax revenues were available for necessary repairs. At the same time, inflation skyrocketed, decreasing funds available for construction. State and local governments were forced to reduce their budgets and workforces for maintenance and repair. The resulting neglect affected all modes of transportation. New York experienced collapsing bridges, congested highways, pothole proliferation, and deteriorating public transportation systems.

In 1983 and 1988, New York State voters approved two bond acts. These would rebuild or repair state highways, parkways, and bridges; eliminate highway-railroad grade crossings; construct and repair rapid transit, commuter rail, rail passenger, and freight facilities; provide capital for airport and aviation projects; and repair and improve ports, marine terminals, canals, and waterways.

Today, and into the near future, federal highway funds are playing a major role in the state transportation picture. The Clean Air Act Amendments of 1990 (CAAA) declared mass transit, and reduced miles traveled, the new order of the day.

The Intermodal Surface Transportation Efficiency Act (ISTEA) became the carrot to the CAAA's stick. This act is intended to bring transportation decisions in line with goals for environmental and community protection, along with economic viability. It shifts the basis for state transportation funding from highway vs. mass transit to a framework based on overall community needs. It requires developing long-range transportation plans that include the impacts of transportation decisions on land use, energy consumption, and community liveability.

With the billions of dollars available from the federal government for highways, bridges, mass transit, and planning, the state must bring its programs into compliance with federal requirements. Both the Clean Air Act Amendments of 1990 and the Intermodal Surface Transportation Efficiency Act renew the focus on metropolitan transportation problems, particularly as they relate to air quality. No longer will our transportation dollars be spent on the cycle of increasing traffic traveling at high speeds, thus causing more highways to be built. The public and local officials must be included in all transportation plans. New development must fit into the principles that incorporate transportation, the environment, and quality of life in communities.

PART FOUR

STATE POLITICS

The United States Constitution makes no mention of political parties, but parties have become essential instruments of representative government, serving as intermediaries between groups of citizens and government institutions. Registered party members band together to advocate their collective preferences for policy choices.

Organized on local, state, and national levels, parties provide the mechanism for the nomination of candidates and the management of their campaigns. In addition, parties play a significant role in staffing the executive branch of government and in building majorities for decision-making by the legislative branch.

12.
ELECTIONS: REGISTRATION AND VOTING*

Americans describe their system of government as a democracy—a system equally committed to majority rule and to the protection of individual and minority rights or, in the words of Abraham Lincoln, "government of the people, by the people, and for the people." But there can be neither majority rule nor government by the people without elections; and to be meaningful, most citizens must participate in these elections.

THE VOTERS

The United States Constitution provides that no state may deny the vote to those 18 years or older. The Federal Voting Rights Act of 1965 and its subsequent amendments prohibit all tests of literacy, and the Supreme Court has held invalid all state qualifications on the length of time an eligible citizen must be a resident in order to vote. A state may, however, permit registration lists to close a reasonable time before an election. New York State closes its registration lists 25 days before the day of the general election. In a presidential election year, New York State residents who move after registration has ended cannot be denied the right to vote for president and vice-president. Such individuals may apply for a special presidential ballot. Although obstacles remain, such as the refusal of some communities to allow

---

*By Lyle Toohey, with special acknowledgment to Peter Kosinski, Special Counsel, New York State Board of Elections.

their college students to vote locally and the unavailability of election day registration, the franchise has effectively been guaranteed to all citizens in New York State.

Voter apathy, however, has made voter turnout in the United States among the lowest of the world's major democracies. We say that Ronald Reagan was elected by a landslide in 1984 because he won approximately 60 percent of the vote, but since only 53 percent of the eligible population voted, Mr. Reagan was actually elected by 31 percent. Looking at it another way, seven out of 10 people either voted for someone else or did not vote at all. The 1992 presidential election marked the first time in history that over 100 million people voted. At an estimated 55 percent, it was the highest recorded turnout in this country in 20 years. Whether 1992 marks the end of a long slide in voter interest and involvement, or is merely an aberration, remains to be seen.

Who Can Vote?

A person is qualified to vote in New York State if he/she is:

- a United States citizen

- 18 years old or older on or before election day

- a resident of New York State and of his/her county, city, town, or village for 30 days before election day

- registered to vote in the election district of residence

People who are on probation and those in prison who are awaiting trial or are serving time for misdemeanors may vote.

Who Cannot Vote?

- convicted felons sentenced to prison until they have completed their sentences and/or parole

- individuals who have been judged legally incompetent by a court

It is a felony to vote illegally or to assist another person to do so.

ELECTIONS

Administration of Elections

In 1974 the New York State Legislature established the New York State Board of Elections, for the first time centralizing responsibility for administering elections in the state. The change largely eliminated diverse interpretations of the law that had produced different registration and voting procedures from county to county. The New York State Board of Elections is an agency of the executive branch.

Local boards of elections in each of the 57 counties and in the city of New York continue the day-to-day supervision of registration and voting, but are guided by the state board which issues advice and direction on the detailed and constantly changing New York State Election Law. Local boards also oversee registration and voting of military voters.

The New York State Board of Elections has specific powers, including:

- issuing instructions and publicly announcing rules and regulations for the "administration of the election process" as well as of campaign practices and campaign financing practices

- visiting, inspecting, and, if necessary, investigating practices of the county and New York City boards of elections

- preparing uniform forms for use by local election officials in the conduct of registration and voting

- reporting annually to the governor and the legislature on the effectiveness of the election laws and making recommendations for reform

- taking "all appropriate steps" to encourage the broadest possible voter participation in elections, including administering the program of registration form distribution by participating state agencies

The state board of elections is also responsible for overseeing the implementation of the National Voter Registration Act of 1993 (Motor Voter), which allows individuals to register to vote when renewing or applying for a driver's license. The act also requires that voter registration services be available at designated government offices.

To enforce its authority, the state board of elections has subpoena power, can bring judicial proceedings in the state Supreme Court, and can refer any of its findings and complaints to the district attorney in the county where any violations of the law or of the board's rules takes place.

The board consists of four salaried members appointed by the governor for two-year, staggered terms. The governor must select each commissioner from a separate list—one each submitted by the state Republican and the Democratic Party chairs; one submitted by the Democratic leaders of the Senate and the Assembly acting jointly; and one selected jointly by the Republican leaders of the two houses.

Local boards of elections are made up of two commissioners, one selected by each of the two major party committees and subsequently appointed by the county legislative body. New York City has 10 commissioners appointed by the city council, one Republican and one Democrat from each of the city's five boroughs.

In the conduct of registration and voting, these boards appoint all election employees on a bipartisan basis, giving the two major parties an equal and exclusive representation in all electoral activity. This bipartisan system is designed to safeguard the electoral process and deter fraud, but critics contend that it shuts out other recognized parties and independents from election administration. Some advocate bringing the conduct of elections under the civil service umbrella and eliminating the party role in administration.

The basic unit of election administration within each county and borough is the election district. There are nearly 15,000 such districts in the state. Most are established by town boards or city councils under election law standards that provide for up to 950 registered voters per district. In New York City, Buffalo, and in the counties of Nassau, Suffolk, and Monroe, election districts are established by the local boards of elections.

Each district has four election inspectors, two from each party, who are in charge of local registration and election day activity. Election inspectors are compensated on an hourly or per diem basis for their service.

Types of Elections in New York State

The political calendar, set each year by the state legislature, is usually built around the date of the primary. It specifies dates for party caucuses, gathering and filing petitions, and sets other deadlines for candidates and party purposes. A copy of this calendar is available at each county board of elections, or it may be obtained from the state board of elections.

A general election is held every year on the first Tuesday after the first Monday in November. Presidential elections are held every fourth year (a leap year). In even-numbered years, elections are held for U.S. Representatives, one-third of the members of the U.S. Senate, state legislators, and some county officials; and every fourth year for governor, lieutenant-governor, comptroller, and attorney general. Most local and city officials are elected in odd-numbered years. Judges may be elected at any election depending on the expiration of their terms. State and local ballot issues may also appear on the ballots at any election.

Primaries are party elections and are held in New York State only when there is a contest within a party for nomination as a candidate to a public office or for election to a party office. Where there is no contest, there is no primary.

The primary is usually held the first Tuesday after the second

Monday in September. The legislature occasionally changes the date
of the primary by amending the election law. The timing of the primary has important political implications: a late primary is thought
to benefit incumbents; early primaries are preferred by challengers
who need time to become known. In presidential election years, an
additional primary is held in the spring for election of delegates to
the national nominating conventions that take place in mid-summer.

When someone in office dies or resigns, a special election may be
held to fill the vacancy. In those cases, the governor sets the date for
the special election.

Village elections are usually held on the third Tuesday in March.
Village residents who are registered with their county board of elections are eligible to vote. In some villages, there may be a village
registration day.

School elections and annual meetings are usually held in May or
June and are governed by the education law rather than the election
law. In central and union free school districts, the school budget
must be submitted to the voters. Members of all boards of education
are elected, except in the cities of New York and Yonkers where they
are appointed. Within New York City, members of community school
boards are elected (see Chapter 9).

Some school districts do not require voter registration; others have
special registration for their own elections or use voter registration
lists from the board of elections. The same voting requirements per-
tain to school elections as to general elections, with one exception. In
New York City, parents of a school child do not have to be citizens to
qualify as voters in a community school board election and may register for such elections in the district where their child attends school
or in the district where they live.

REGISTRATION PROCEDURES

New York State has a system of permanent personal registration
(PPR). This enables a voter, after initially registering, to remain per-

manently registered to vote unless he or she moves or fails to vote in at least one general, special, primary, or village election during a five-year period which ends in a presidential election year. In that case, the voter will be notified by the local board of elections that he/she is not registered and must respond to the notice by re-registering in order to vote.

In New York State, voters may register by mail or in person. Voters may obtain mail registration forms from their local board of elections, town or city clerks, political parties, public libraries, post offices, various state agencies, or the League of Women Voters. The completed forms must be postmarked no later than 25 days before the election and received by the local board of elections no later than 22 days before the election.

Voters may register in person during normal business hours at their local board of elections any day, except on the day of an election. Voters may also register in person during a local registration day in late September or early October if one is held. Local boards have the option of not holding a local registration day in years when there is no presidential election. In presidential election years, local boards are required to schedule two local registration days. City, town, or village clerks are responsible for designating and announcing places for local registration, but generally these are local polling places.

The National Voter Registration Act, known as "Motor Voter," was passed by Congress in 1993. The state expects to adopt full implementing legislation shortly. The act provides for simultaneous application for voter registration with an application for a driver's license and permits mail registration as well as application at public assistance agencies. It not only aims to make voter registration easier, but to promote statewide uniform recordkeeping of the voter registration rolls.

The election law makes special provisions for absentee registration for resident patients at veterans hospitals and for members of the armed services and their families.

In New York State, a voter may choose to enroll in one of the five recognized parties: Democratic, Republican, Conservative, Right to Life, and Liberal. A voter may decline to enroll in any party. Party enrollment and registration lists are available for public inspection at the county boards of elections. Only enrolled members of a party can vote in that party's primary election. Registered voters may change enrollment at any time, but change of enrollment goes into effect only after the next general election. On election day, registered voters may vote for any candidate of any party.

VOTING

Election Day Procedures

Polls are open from 6 a.m. to 9 p.m. across the state for the general election, and from 12 noon until 9 p.m. for the primary (except in New York City and Nassau, Suffolk, Erie, Westchester, Rockland, Orange, and Ulster Counties, where polls are open from 6 a.m. to 9 p.m). Electioneering is prohibited within a distance of 100 feet from each polling place. The election inspectors are responsible for maintaining order and for carrying out the provisions of the election law.

It is the responsibility of a city or town council to provide enough voting machines to all the election districts within the city or town. In a general election, districts (except those in New York City) that contain more than 800 voters shall have two voting machines. In the primary election, voting machines may be provided.

Inspectors must give instructions on the use of the voting machine to those voters who request it, and each polling place is required to have a sample ballot. Voters who require assistance in operating the voting machine because of a physical disability or illiteracy may receive help from anyone of their choice, except an employer or a union representative.

Voters who are refused the right to vote at the polls have two options:

1. They may request and sign an affidavit that they are registered to vote in that election district. They can then vote by paper ballot. Each ballot will be returned to the board of elections and counted only if the board records uphold the voter's affidavit. If a ballot is not counted, the board notifies that voter that she or he is not registered and sends a mail registration form.

2. They may appeal to a state Supreme Court justice or to a judge of the County Court for court orders requiring that they be permitted to vote. These courts must stay in session during election hours to receive such appeals, which take precedence over other litigation. With a court order, the voters vote on the voting machine.

Candidates have a specified period after the vote has been tallied to challenge the count. The state Supreme Court may order machines impounded and a recount undertaken. Final results are officially announced by the state or local board of elections.

Absentee Voting

Voters may request absentee ballots for general elections, village elections, primaries, and for special elections called by the governor. Some school districts permit absentee voting for school board elections but not for school budgets or other ballot issues, nor for special school district elections.

Registered voters who are ill, physically disabled, or away from the county of residence on election day are eligible for absentee ballots. Absentee ballot applications are available from county boards of elections until the day before the election. Voters may also apply during local registration days.

Voters who claim permanent illness or disability may request that absentee ballots be mailed to them before each election by filing letters with their local boards of elections, describing the particulars of their illnesses or disabilities. The local board of elections will investigate and, if satisfied, will mark the voter's registration records "Per-

manently Disabled" and send an absentee ballot to the voter prior to
each election.

Completed absentee ballot applications must be postmarked no
later than the seventh day before the election or hand delivered to
the county board of elections no later than the day before the election. Completed absentee ballots must be hand delivered to the county
board of elections by the close of polls on election day or postmarked
no later than the day before the election.

FAIR CAMPAIGN PRACTICES

At present, the laws in New York State do not adequately protect
against unfair campaign practices. Although a "Fair Campaign Code"
was adopted in 1975, portions of it were declared unconstitutional
by the United States Supreme Court because it did not provide for
judicial review of administrative decisions made by the New York
State Board of Elections. Since then, legislation for a new code that
would meet constitutional guidelines has been introduced repeatedly, but the New York State Legislature has failed to adopt it.

Some of the practices that the code would prohibit are deliberate
misrepresentation of a candidate's viewpoints or actions, misuse of
the results of opinion polls, fraudulent or untrue endorsements of a
candidate, doctored photographs or writings of a candidate, and
political espionage.

DID YOU KNOW . . . In some counties, volunteer Fair Campaign Practices Committees receive and rule on complaints of
unfair practices by candidates.

13.
RUNNING FOR OFFICE*

DEFINITION OF A PARTY

A recognized political party, according to the New York State Election Law, is one in which its candidate for governor won at least 50,000 votes in the previous gubernatorial election. There are now five recognized parties in New York State: Democratic, Republican, Conservative, Right to Life, and Liberal. The order in which they are listed on the ballot is determined by the number of votes each received in the previous gubernatorial election. A recognized party is expected to maintain a year-round organization and participate in primaries. Other political groups, which the election law calls "independent bodies," may organize to run one or more candidates in a single election.

By law and by custom, political parties play an intrinsic role in American government. Their power, like the government's, stems from the people, although the constitution of the United States makes no mention of them. Like the government, political parties are organized on local, state, and national levels. Political parties have become essential instruments of representative government, serving as intermediaries between groups of citizens and governmental institutions. Through them, registered party members band together to advocate their collective preferences for policy choices and candidates. Parties provide the mechanism for the nomination of candi-

*By Susan Hughson.

dates and the management of their general election campaigns. In
addition, parties play a significant role in staffing the executive and
legislative branches of government and in building majorities for
decision-making by the legislative branch.

BACKGROUND OF POLITICAL PARTIES

Although there is some evidence that the recent period of party
decline has been arrested in New York State and throughout the nation, political parties are certainly no longer as significant and influ-
ential as they once were. Nationally, about 30 percent of the registered voters consider themselves as "independents"; that is, they
choose not to belong to any party. And those who do belong often
seem to be less partisan, less party-oriented, than in the past. Nevertheless, the parties continue to perform important functions linking
the citizen to government.

There are many reasons why people choose not to belong to a
party. Subversion of the political process with "Watergate"-type
abuses from the presidential level on down have turned many away
from the parties. Media and public relations advisors, able to package a candidate as a marketable item, have partly replaced the party
as the originator of campaign strategy. Polls, rather than the party
platform, are now often the source of a candidate's positions. The
mass media are replacing parties in their role of informing the electorate about the candidates. Finally, personality politics and media-
centered campaigns siphon workers and contributors away from the
party.

Many voters today are also impatient and frustrated with the loose
consensus politics that has traditionally held together each of the two
major parties. Political activists who focus their energy on single-
issue organizations tend to weaken the major parties by depriving
them of members with important political know-how and financial
support, and make it more difficult for parties to develop broad, in-
clusive platforms.

Surprisingly perhaps, the one-man/one-vote principle, which has improved the equality of our representation in local, state, and national legislative bodies, has also done its share to undermine party organizations. Districts created solely on the basis of population tend to produce candidates with few ties to existing party organizations which continue to be structured along town, city, and county lines.

Minor parties may provide the margin of victory in a close contest by cross-endorsing a major party nominee, thus gaining influence greater than their actual membership warrants. The 1992 party enrollment figures in New York State may provide some perspective here: Democrats, 4.2 million; Republicans, 2.9 million; not enrolled (independents), 1.8 million; Conservatives, 130,000; Liberals, 73,000; and Right to Life, 34,000. These numbers prove that New York is essentially a partisan, two-party state.

At one time, the party that prevailed in an election was represented in government not only by the candidates it placed in office, but by the people it recommended for appointment to government posts, both small and large. At its best, this patronage system generated people to carry out the policies of the party that the voters had elected. It also provided rewards and incentives for those who had supported the party and volunteered their efforts. At its worst, the system substituted party loyalty for competence as a qualification for a government job. In either case, it was the life of the party. Today, much of the government bureaucracy is ruled by Civil Service examinations rather than the patronage system; thus, the parties have fewer rewards to offer those who serve them. Local party organizations continue, however, to provide opportunities for involvement in civic affairs and for influencing public policy and the selection of candidates for public office.

In recent years, campaign finance laws (see end of chapter) have subjected parties and candidates to stricter accounting and disclosure regulations. Changes in party rules assure all factions a stronger role in decision-making, from local and state primaries to presidential nominating conventions. Paradoxically, with all their problems—or because of them—parties today are more accessible than ever before to the influence of voters who wish to use the political vehicle they provide.

PARTY ENROLLMENT

Enrolled party members are entitled to vote in that party's primary elections, sign nominating petitions, hold party office, and participate in party caucuses.

During local registration, or when registering by mail, voters may enroll in the party of their choice, may choose not to enroll in any party, or may change their party enrollment. Change of enrollment goes into effect only after the following general election. On election day, registered voters may vote as they please.

PARTY ORGANIZATION

Wards and the election districts within them are the building blocks of party organization. Consisting of no more than 950 registered voters each, they are the smallest political units in the state. They are the scene of the proverbial grassroots party activity, where the party faithful work to win votes for the party's candidates and to get voters to the polls. Except in the cities of New York and Buffalo, and in the counties of Monroe, Nassau, and Suffolk (where election districts are drawn by the boards of elections), these units are established by town boards and city councils. The small size of the election districts gives parties great flexibility to organize as political units within any district from which candidates are elected to public office, such as state legislative or congressional districts.

The Local Party Committee

Enrolled party members within each election district choose two committee members, usually one man and one woman (except where party rules permit the election of three or four from each district). Committee members must be residents of the Assembly district in which their election districts are located.

Together, all the committee members choose the local (city, town, or village) party chairperson and other officers. This committee is then responsible for party activity in the community: obtaining signatures for petitions, registering voters, getting out the vote, raising money, and conducting local campaigns. For purely local offices in cities or towns, the chairperson and executive members of the city or town committee usually select the candidate who is then endorsed by the whole committee. Candidates for town and village offices are in some cases chosen at party caucuses open to all party members.

Local party organizations may be aided by local political clubs that are semisocial, semipolitical centers for party members. Although it has no official party status or role, in many places a club serves as the local campaign headquarters and as a meeting place for both party leaders and for rank-and-file members. It is the place to which a party member traditionally has come to seek advice on ways to obtain help or information from public officials.

The County Committee

The county party organization is the basic unit of party machinery and, as such, is the base of party power. Within limits, these county organizations may make party rules to govern their operations. There may be a good deal of variation among and within parties from one county to another. Committee members in all the election districts in the county make up the county committee, which in turn elects county party officers.

Candidates for county-wide offices, including county-level judgeships, the state legislature, and the U.S. House of Representatives, are generally endorsed by the county committee acting as a whole or by the county executive committee, according to party rules in a particular county. Where a congressional or state legislative district crosses county lines, the committees of all involved counties must endorse the candidates. Except in New York City (the state's only city that contains more than one county), each county organization has an executive committee made up of city, ward, and town chairpersons, plus other elected officers.

Party Organization in New York City

In New York City, there is no formal citywide political organization, but each of its five counties has an executive committee composed of Assembly district leaders and other officers. The district leaders are elected directly by the enrolled voters of the party. This executive committee, or in some cases the whole county committee, elects the county chairperson.

The Assembly district leaders and committees handle nominations for the state Assembly and wield considerable influence over the choice of candidates for the state senate, U.S. House of Representatives, and major city offices. As in other parts of the state, the county party organization, through its leaders, exercises political power through patronage and the influence it exerts on elected officials.

The State Committee

State committee members are elected for two-year terms from such districts as the rules of the party may provide. County leaders have a major voice in selecting the persons who will run for state committee positions in each district.

The state committee elects a state chairperson and an executive committee; it adopts a party platform, raises money for the party, designates the party's candidates for statewide offices, chooses the chairperson and delegates-at-large for national party nominating conventions at which the party's presidential candidates are named, and selects the party's slate of presidential electors. The state committee also chooses several men and women to serve on the national party committee. Party committees at the state and lower levels are elected at primary elections if there is a contest. Party officers, who are the most visible party functionaries, are then named by the committees.

The National Committee

Essentially, national parties consist of their national committee, national chairperson and staff, their elected and appointed public officials, their party members, and a quadrennial presidential nominating convention attended by party delegates from each state.

HOW THE PARTY CHOOSES ITS CANDIDATES

Party organizations have the initial role in nominating persons for public as well as for party office. Normally the party leadership at the appropriate level indicates its preferred choices and causes designating petitions to be circulated on behalf of its candidates. When there is no challenge to the leadership choice, the filing of that candidate's petitions constitutes election to party office or nomination to public office. If there is any opposition within the party to this choice, challengers may circulate their own petitions and the outcome is settled at a primary election. The election law specifies the dates for circulating and filing the petitions and the numbers of signatures required for candidates in each size district (for example, fewer signatures are required for petitions in an Assembly than in a congressional district).

Primary elections and the circulation of petitions have these aspects in common: only voters enrolled in the party may vote in its primary, and only enrolled party members may circulate or sign petitions for a party candidate.

A special provision that applies only to New York City requires persons seeking nomination to citywide offices to capture at least 40 percent of the party vote in the primary. If no candidate does so, the nomination will be decided in a runoff primary between the two front-runners.

Although regulations surrounding primary contests are detailed and complex, the system does permit an appeal to the members of the party by any group or individual in case of disagreement over actions of the leadership.

Nomination to Statewide Office

New York State has a challenge primary system for selecting party candidates for statewide public office. Candidates may be designated by a majority vote of the state party committee. Any candidate who receives 25 percent of the vote of the state committee, however, may challenge the party designation in a statewide primary.

Even candidates who fail to win this percentage may force a statewide primary by gathering the signatures of 15,000 enrolled voters, with a minimum of 100 signatures per district in at least half of the state's congressional districts. This alternative clearly adds to the expenses of the challenger. The relative ease in which this system affords candidates a direct appeal to party voters has encouraged a growing number of candidates to vie for the support of the overall party membership. The challenge primary system in New York State has thus reinforced a tendency for political aspirants to act independently of the established party organization and to draw and divert strength from party organizations.

INDEPENDENT NOMINATIONS

A person does not have to belong to, or have the backing of, a recognized party to run for office. Evidence of this fact is the 1992 presidential candidacy of Ross Perot. Mr. Perot ran as an independent, not as a member of a party.

New York State election law spells out the manner in which independent groups may organize to nominate candidates by circulating petitions to put their names on the ballot. Because independent candidates are not involved in primaries, a much larger number of signatures is required for their petitions than for regular party-designating petitions. Independent petitions are circulated during specified periods after the party petition period, and a candidate who has failed to win the party designation may subsequently file to run as an independent. In addition, a voter can vote for candidates not listed on the ballot by writing in his or her name.

FINANCING CAMPAIGNS

Despite numerous complaints about the length, quality, cost, and many other aspects of political campaigns, campaign finance is one of the few areas where candidates have any legal restrictions. In recent years, television, polling, sampling, direct mail, and other modern campaign techniques that candidates use to reach enormous numbers of people have all helped to escalate the cost of running for office. To prevent candidates from relying too heavily on large donors seeking influence, the New York State Board of Elections was established to supervise campaign financing, as well as to administer registration and voting procedures. Soon after the law was framed, courts struck down limits on spending as an unconstitutional barrier to freedom of speech. However, limits on contributions are still in place.

The maximum amount that a single contributor may give to a candidate running for statewide office (governor, lieutenant-governor, comptroller, and attorney general) is equal to one-half cent per enrolled voter in the primary, up to $12,000; and in the general election, up to $25,000. The limit on the amount that members of a candidate's family can give collectively is two-and-a-half cents per registered voter.

In primary, special, or general elections for local offices (county, city, town, or village), a single donor may contribute up to five cents per voter in the district or $50,000, whichever is less, except that the candidate's family may give 25 cents per voter or $100,000, whichever is less. The U.S. Supreme Court has ruled that no limit may be put on the amount that a candidate and spouse can contribute to the campaign.

The total that any one donor may contribute in a single year to all political campaigns is set at $150,000; corporations are permitted to contribute $5,000 to all campaigns in a calendar year. However, these limits are often misunderstood, and there is no centralized system for keeping track of contributions.

The law sets other limits on campaign financing, including stringent reporting requirements on all campaign receipts and expenditures; provisions to identify all contributors; and prohibitions against accepting any contribution of more than $100, except by check or other signed draft.

Campaign financing reform, including public funding, continues to remain an area of concern and controversy at all levels. Political Action Committees (PACs) multiplied and gained in influence after national campaign finance legislation was passed in 1974. Although their activities and finances are regulated, they provide a mechanism whereby any group, including business corporations and labor unions, may channel funds to a candidate's election campaign or to a campaign on a ballot issue.

PART FIVE

ACCESS TO GOVERNMENT

Across the country in the early 1970s, public concern over the conduct of public officials generated new interest in open government. This concern gave rise to a number of "sunshine" laws and policies governing access to information, open meetings, and regulations of lobbyists. More recently, considerable concern has been expressed in relation to establishing ethical standards for government officials.

In New York State, the "Freedom of Information Law" went into effect in 1974. Three years later the "Open Meetings Law" took effect and the Committee on Public Access to Records was established to oversee the implementation of both laws. In 1983 the committee's name was changed to Committee on Open Government. This committee is composed of 11 members, five from government and six from the public. The five government members include the lieutenant-governor, the secretary of state, the commissioner of general services, the director of the budget, and one elected local government official appointed by the governor. The public members are appointed by the governor and the leaders of the Senate and the Assembly. Two of the public members must be or have been representatives of the news media.

The Committee on Open Government, which operates under the New York State Department of State, furnishes advice to government agencies, the public, and the news media; issues regulations and advisory opinions; reviews the operation of the law; and reports its observations and recommendations annually to the governor and the legislature.

Those needing advice regarding either the Freedom of Information Law or the Open Meetings Law should contact: Committee on Open Government, New York State Department of State, 162 Washington Avenue, Albany, NY 12231.

14.
ACCESS TO GOVERNMENT*

FREEDOM OF INFORMATION LAW

DID YOU KNOW . . . that the public is entitled to access to all public documents, except those that deal with personal matters?

The Freedom of Information Law assures public access to government records. With certain exceptions, state and local agencies must make their records available to the public, and the law also requires that any accessible records filed or used in local government may be inspected and copied by the public. (Fees for copies ordinarily cannot exceed 25 cents per copy.) The law defines the term "agency" to include all units of state and local government—state agencies, public corporations (school boards, city councils, and town and village boards), and authorities—as well as any other governmental entity performing a governmental function for the state or a unit of local government. The term "agency," however, does not include the state legislature or the courts. Exempted from public scrutiny are matters of an intimate personal nature, such as medical histories, law enforcement records, credit records, and personal references.

In some cases, people seeking information from government agencies are refused the information they request. If initially denied ac-

*By Evelyn Stock, with special acknowledgment to Robert Freeman, Executive Director, Commission on Open Government.

cess, they have the right to appeal to the head of the agency. If they feel the agency is wrong to refuse the information, they may sue the agency and let the court decide whether or not the information should be made available. At one time, some people were unable to take advantage of the intent of the law because they could not afford the cost of going to court. The law was amended in 1982 to permit the court to award reasonable attorney's fees and other court costs to plaintiffs able to prove the information should have been provided. The agency must then pay these costs, but this is relatively rare.

OPEN MEETINGS LAW

DID YOU KNOW . . . that the public is entitled to attend all public meetings and hear the deliberations?

The purpose of the Open Meetings Law is to assure that government business is conducted openly. The law gives the public the right to attend meetings of public bodies, listen to the discussions, and watch the decision-making process in action. The law, however, does not guarantee members of the public the right to speak at these meetings.

In the original version of the law, the definition of the term "meetings" was vague. Later, court interpretations of the law defined meetings to mean "the official convening of a public body for the purpose of conducting public business." The law applies to all public bodies, and the term "public body" is defined to cover entities consisting of two or more people that conduct public business and perform a governmental function for the state, for an agency of the state, or for such public corporations as city councils, town boards, village boards, school boards, zoning boards, commissions, legislative bodies, and committees and subcommittees of all those groups.

The law provides for closed or "executive" sessions under certain circumstances. Executive sessions are not separate from open meetings, but are a portion of an open meeting from which the public may be excluded. To close a meeting for executive session, a public body must take several steps. First, a motion must be made during an open meeting to enter into executive session. Second, the motion must identify the general area or areas of the subject or subjects to be considered in executive session. Third, the motion must be carried by a majority vote of the total membership of a public body.

It is important to know, however, that a public body cannot close its doors to the public to discuss any subject it chooses, since the law also limits the matter that may be discussed in executive session. Only certain subjects may be considered privately. These include matters of public safety, criminal investigation, current or pending litigation, collective negotiations involving public employee unions, land acquisition, and personal privacy.

The law also requires that notice of the time and place of all meetings be made public in advance of the meeting. Further, minutes of all meetings must be made available. Minutes of open meetings must include a record of all matters formally voted upon, as well as how each member of the body voted. Minutes of executive sessions are required only if action was taken during the session.

The Open Meetings Law does not apply to judicial proceedings, political party committees and caucuses, or matters made confidential by federal or state law.

The exemptions of political party committees and caucuses from the Open Meetings Law is a cause of concern for proponents of open government. The original law was vague on what matters could be discussed privately in meetings of government officials who are members of the same party. Over time, the courts decided that the intent of the law was to allow only discussion of party business in private and to require discussion of any subject pertaining to public business in public. In 1985 the state legislature amended the law to permit party caucuses to discuss any matters they chose, including public business, with the result that matters of public concern can be discussed in private by the majority party, with only the vote taken in open meetings. This amendment makes it possible for a legislative body effectively to eliminate public observance of its decision-making process.

LOBBYING REGULATIONS

> DID YOU KNOW . . . that lobbyists must register each year and declare how much money is spent on their lobbying activities?

Lobbyists are persons who seek to influence legislators in regard to proposed laws. They cannot be members of either house. They may represent a specific business or labor group, a citizen organization, or a particular political ideology. In many ways, lobbyists can perform a useful function by supplying legislators with information and technical advice on bills and alerting them to the interests of certain groups. Legislators, however, can be vulnerable to representatives of those special interests that can commit large sums of money to further certain legislative objectives. The purpose of lobbying regulations is to give the public access to information about such efforts. The law requires any lobbyist or organization that plans to spend more than $2,000 toward influencing legislation to register annually and to file quarterly itemized reports of expenditures. A Temporary State Commission on Regulation of Lobbying oversees the reporting procedure.

ETHICS

A new ethics code for state officials and employees was passed in 1987. It covers statewide elected officials, state officers and employees, and legislators and legislative employees. For certain purposes, it also covers political party chairs. The law also required local governments with populations of more than 50,000 to have their own codes of ethics in place by 1991. The Ethics Law contains a multitude of provisions. Among other things, it requires financial disclosure by the people it covers. Additionally, it prohibits them from making appearances or providing legal services for private clients in almost all cases involving state agencies, and also prohibits them from selling goods or services to state agencies for amounts greater than $75.

A "revolving door" provision, covering former state officers and employees, bars them from rendering services on behalf of private clients before their former state agencies for a period of two years from the time of leaving government service. However, there is no law barring former legislators from lobbying, provided they are not paid lobbyists. Although the law is specific on a large number of things, many people feel that it still contains "ominous gaps and loopholes." To overcome these perceived weaknesses, many amendments to the law continue to be proposed.

APPENDIX:

New York State Executive, Judicial, Legislative, and Administrative Departments and Offices

EXECUTIVE:

Governor
Executive Chamber
State Capitol
Albany, NY 12224
518-474-8390

Lieutenant-Governor
State Capitol
Room 326
Albany, NY 12224
518-474-4623

Comptroller
Gov. Alfred E. Smith
  Office Building
Albany, NY 12202
518-474-4044

Attorney General
State Capitol
Albany, NY 12224
518-474-7124

Board of Elections
Swan Street Building
Core 1
Empire State Plaza
Albany, NY 12223
518-474-6220

Commission on Judicial Conduct
38-40 State Street
Albany, NY 12207
518-474-5617

Consumer Protection Board
One Commerce Plaza
Albany, NY 12210
518-474-8583

Council on Children and Families
Empire State Plaza
Corning Tower, 28th Floor
Albany, NY 12223
518-473-3652

Council on the Arts
915 Broadway, 7th Floor
New York, NY 10010
212-614-2900

Crime Victims Compensation Board
845 Central Avenue
Albany, NY 12206
518-457-8727

Division for Women
4 Empire State Plaza
  (Agency Building)
Albany, NY 12223
518-474-3612

Division for Youth
52 Washington Avenue
Rensselaer, NY 12144
518-473-7793

Division of the Budget
State Capitol
Albany, NY 12224
518-473-9389

Division of Criminal
  Justice Services
Executive Park Tower
Stuyvescent Plaza
Albany, NY 12203
518-457-6113

Division of Housing and
  Community Renewal
1 Fordham Plaza
Bronx, NY 10548
718-519-5789;

Hampton Plaza
38-40 State Street
Albany, NY 12210
518-473-2517;
1-800-432-4210

Division of Human Rights
55 West 125th Street
New York, NY 10025
212-961-8400;

Gov. Alfred W. Smith
  Office Building
Albany, NY 12202
518-474-2705

Energy Office
Empire State Plaza
  (Agency Building 2)
Albany, NY 12223
518-473-4375;
1-800-423-7283

Office for the Aging
Empire State Plaza
  (Agency Building 2)
Albany, NY 12223
518-474-5731;
1-800-342-9871

Office for Prevention of
  Domestic Violence
52 Washington Avenue
Rensselaer, NY 12144
518-486-6262

Office of Alcoholism and
  Substance Abuse Services
1450 Western Avenue
Albany, NY 12203
518-473-3460

Office of Mental Health
44 Holland Avenue
Albany, NY 12229
518-474-2568

Office of Mental Retardation and
  Developmental Disabilities
44 Holland Avenue
Albany, NY 12208
518-473-9689

Office of Parks and Recreation
  and Historic Preservation
Empire State Plaza
  (Agency Building 1)
Albany, NY 12238
518-474-0456

JUDICIAL:

Office of Court Administration
4 Empire State Plaza, 20th Floor
  (Agency Building)
Albany, NY 12223
518-474-1038;

270 Broadway
New York, NY 10007
212-417-5900

Chief Judge of the Court of Appeals
Court Appeals Hall
Eagle Street
Albany, NY 12207
518-455-7740

LEGISLATIVE:

New York State Assembly
Legislative Office Building
Albany, NY 12248
518-455-4100

New York State Senate
Legislative Office Building
Albany, NY 12247
518-455-2800

ADMINISTRATIVE
 DEPARTMENTS
 AND OFFICES:

Department of Agriculture
 and Markets
Capitol Plaza
1 Winner's Circle
Albany, NY 12235
518-474-2121

Department of Banking
2 Rector Street
New York, NY 10016
212-618-6642;

194 Washington Avenue
Albany, NY 12210
1-800-522-7124

Department of Civil Service
State Campus
 (Civil Service Building)
Albany, NY 12239
518-474-2121
Handicapped Employment:
1-800-635-6333

Department of Commerce
1 Commerce Plaza
Albany, NY 12210
518-474-6812

Department of Correctional Services
State Campus
 (Correctional Services Building)
Albany, NY 12226
518-474-2121

Department of Education
Cultural Education Center
Albany, NY 12234
518-474-3852

Department of Environmental
 Conservation
50 Wolf Road
Albany, NY 12205
518-474-2121

Department of Health
Empire State Plaza
 (Tower Building)
Albany, NY 12223
518-474-2121

Department of Insurance
160 West Broadway
New York, NY 10013
212-602-0434;

Empire State Plaza
 (Agency Building 1)
Albany, NY 12257
518-474-6600
General Information:
1-800-342-3736

Department of Labor
State Campus
 (Building 12)
Albany, NY 12240
518-457-9000

Department of Law
State Capitol
Albany, NY 12224
518-474-7124

Department of Motor Vehicles
Empire State Plaza
   (Swan Street Building)
Albany, NY 12228
518-473-5595

Department of Public Service
Empire State Plaza
   (Agency Building 3)
Albany, NY 12223
518-474-2530

Department of Social Services
40 North Pearl Street
Albany, NY 12207
518-473-3170;
1-800-342-3720

Department of State
162 Washington Avenue
Albany, NY 12210
518-474-4752; 518-474-4750
Ombudsman:
1-800-828-2338
*Committee on Open
   Government:*
518-474-2518

**Department of Taxation
   and Finance**
State Campus
   (Building 9)
Albany, NY 12227
Tax Information:
1-800-225-5829
Tax Forms:
1-800-462-8100
Tax Refunds:
1-800-443-3200

Department of Transportation
State Campus
   (Building 5)
Albany, NY 12232
518-457-6195

GLOSSARY

absentee ballot: an official ballot used by a voter who is unable to go to the polls on election day because of absence or illness.

acid rain: precipitation that carries air pollution to the ground.

acquittal: a court's decision that an accused person is not guilty.

act: a law made by a governing body, such as a state legislature.

administration: the governor, governor's staff, and other officials who take leadership roles in the executive branch of government.

administrative law: rules and regulations issued by government agencies.

advisory opinion: an opinion by an attorney general regarding the constitutionality of a law.

affirmative action: a policy or program for correcting the effects of discrimination in the employment or education of members of certain groups, such as women, blacks, and Hispanics.

amendment: a revision or addition proposed or made in a bill, law, or constitution.

annexation: the expansion of municipal boundaries to include a bordering area.

appellate jurisdiction: the right of a higher court to review a decision of a lower court.

apportionment: proportional distribution of the number of members of the U.S. House of Representatives, New York State Assembly, and New York State Senate, on the basis of population.

aquifer: underground geological formations that store and transmit significant quantities of ground water.

arraignment: the formal reading in open court of charges against a defendant.

assembly: a body of lawmakers in state government; the Assembly is one of two houses in New York State government.

assessment: an estimate of the value of property for purposes of taxation.

assessor: a local government official who inspects property and estimates its value.

at-large: a system of election by which all voters of a city or town elect government officials.

attorney general: the chief legal officer of state government.

bail: money exchanged for release of an arrested person as guarantee of that person's appearance for trial.

bench trial: trial by a judge rather than by a jury.

bicameral: having two legislative houses.

bilingual education: classroom instruction in a student's native language as well as English.

bill: a proposed law that is being considered by a legislature.

bill of rights: constitutional list of the basic civil liberties of citizens.

bipartisan: consisting of or supported by members of two major parties.

block grant: a grant from the federal government channeling money to a state (or from the state to a local municipality) for general purposes.

board of elections: a governmental agency that monitors political elections to ensure that election laws are enforced.

board of equalization: a group established by a government to ensure fair property taxes.

bond: a loan to the government by private citizens or corporations.

brief: a written document presenting one side of a court case.

budget: a plan for spending money over a certain period of time; an itemized summary of expenditures and income for a given period.

bureaucracy: the agencies and offices that take part in managing the government.

calendar: a formal schedule of bills to be considered by a legislature; a schedule of cases to come before a court (also called a **docket**).

capital punishment: the death penalty.

caucus: a meeting of the members of a political party to nominate candidates to decide party policies.

census: an official count of the population.

charge: to accuse a person formally of an illegal act.

charter: a legal document granted by a state creating a government entity, a college, a bank, or a public authority.

checks and balances: a system under which each branch of government limits the power of the other branches.

chief executive: the official who runs or administers a government. The governor is the chief executive of New York State.

citizen: a person entitled by birth or naturalization to the protection of a government or a nation.

citizenship: the special status, including rights and responsibilities, possessed by a person by virtue of birth or naturalization.

city manager: professional employed by a city council to oversee the city's operations.

civil law: the body of law that deals with the relations between people. Also called **private law.**

civil rights: the right of every citizen to be treated equally under the law and to have equality of opportunity.

civil service: the system by which public employees are hired and promoted on the basis of merit rather than because of political party affiliation (the "**spoils system**").

code: a system of regulations and rules of procedure.

code of ethics: rules and guidelines for behavior of government officials.

collective bargaining: negotiations between a union and an employer to determine wages, hours, and working conditions.

commission: a group of people officially authorized to perform certain duties or functions.

committee: a group of legislators who meet to consider bills in a single area, for example, agriculture, appropriations, commerce, or election law.

comptroller: chief financial officer of the state.

constituency: the people whom elected officials represent and to whom they are directly accountable.

constitution: a document outlining the basic form and rules of a government.

convention: a formal meeting of members, representatives, or delegates of a group, such as a political party.

council manager: a form of municipal government in which the voters elect a council to make policy, and the council appoints a manager to execute the policy.

county: a municipal corporation, established by the state legislature, with geographical jurisdiction, powers, and fiscal capacity to provide a wide range of services to residents.

county executive: an official, usually elected, who heads the executive branch of county government.

county manager: professional manager appointed by the governing board of a county to supervise day-to-day operations.

county seat: a town or city containing the county government's offices and buildings.

criminal law: the body of law that specifies offenses against the public and the penalties for committing those offenses.

debt limit: a constitutional borrowing limit placed on municipalities whereby they may borrow up to a set percentage of their assessed valuation of real property.

deficit: the amount by which a sum of money falls short of the required amount.

deficit spending: the practice of spending funds in excess of income, especially by a government.

democracy: rule by the people.

docket: *see* **calendar.**

district attorney: chief prosecuting attorney of a county or state; an elected official.

due process of law: fair and predictable procedures to ensure the fair treatment of those accused of crimes.

ecology: science of the relationships between organisms and their environment.

election: the act of selecting public officials by vote.

election district: basic unit of election administration, having no more than 950 registered voters in it; district lines are set by the municipality.

electorate: people who are legally eligible to vote in an election.

emissions: pollutants released into the air, especially by the internal combustion engines of automobiles, trucks, and buses.

enabling act: a provision added to a constitutional amendment authorizing the legislature to pass whatever laws are necessary to make the amendment effective.

endorsement: expressing public support for a candidate for political office.

equalization rate: a formula to create equity in tax rates among multiple units of local government when the assessed valuations bear a varying relationship to full value. This formula is used in county tax assessment and in school districts that cover more than one community.

executive: the branch of federal, state, or local government that is responsible for putting laws into effect. The chief executive of New York State is the governor.

executive budget: a state budget that is prepared under the direct supervision of the governor.

executive order: a rule or regulation issued by the governor to help enforce a law.

felony: a serious crime punishable by more than one year in prison.

fiscal policy: a governmental tool for influencing the economy by changing levels of taxing and spending.

fiscal year: the 12-month period for which a government plans the use of its funds.

flat grant: the minimum amount of state aid to education given to all school districts regardless of their wealth.

fossil fuel: an energy source, such as coal, oil, or natural gas, formed millions of years ago from decomposed plants and animals.

franchise: the right to vote.

GAAP (General Accepted Accounting Principles): sets forth uniform minimum standards and guidelines for financial accounting and reporting.

general election: an election involving most or all voters of a state in selecting candidates and/or deciding ballot issues; held on the first Tuesday after the first Monday in November.

general welfare: the well-being of a society as a whole (see also **social welfare**).

gerrymander: setting district boundary lines to favor a particular candidate, political party, or group.

govern: to make and administer the public policy and affairs of state.

government: the people and institutions with the authority to establish and enforce laws and public policy.

governor: the chief executive of a state.

grand jury: a group of people who decide whether there is sufficient evidence to hold a person for a criminal trial.

grant-in-aid: monies given on a matching basis to a state or a local government by the national or state government for a particular program or project.

hand down: to announce or deliver.

Home Rule: the principle that a locality should have complete self-government of its internal affairs.

hydroelectric power: power produced by the energy of falling water (channeled through dams).

immunity: the promise of legal authorities that the testimony given by witnesses will not be used to prosecute them for crimes.

impeach: to accuse a public official of misconduct before an appropriate tribunal.

inalienable rights: rights that cannot be denied.

income tax: a tax on a person's income.

incumbent: a person who holds political office.

independent: a person who has not enrolled in a political party.

indictment: a formal statement presented by a prosecuting attorney charging a person with committing a crime.

inflation: a persistent, substantial rise in the general price level, resulting in a fall of purchasing power.

infrastructure: the basic installations and facilities, such as roads, bridges, schools, and transportation systems, of a community or state. Infrastructure neglect over several decades has led to the deterioration of some of these systems, necessitating costly repairs.

initiative: the procedure by which citizens can propose a law by petition and ensure its submission to the electorate.

interstate: pertaining to two or more states.

intrastate: pertaining to or existing within the boundaries of one state.

Jacksonian democracy: the movement toward greater citizen participation in government.

joint session: a session in which both legislative houses meet together.

judge: a public official authorized to make decisions on cases of law.

judicial: the branch of government that decides laws have been broken and that punishes lawbreakers.

judicial review: the power of the courts to decide whether certain laws and acts of governmental officials are consistent with the ideas of the constitution.

jurisdiction: authority vested in the court to hear certain cases.

labor: the human resources needed to produce goods and services.

law: all the rule of conduct established by a government and applicable to a people, whether in the form of legislation or of custom.

legislative: the branch of government that makes laws.

legislator: a person who makes or votes on laws; a member of legislative body.

legislature: the lawmaking branch of government.

lobbyist: a representative of an organization or group that attempts to influence laws.

logrolling: practice by which lawmakers agree to vote for each other's bills.

magistrate: a minor official with limited judicial powers, such as a justice of the peace or judge of a police court.

majority rule: the principle by which people agree to abide by decisions on which more than half of them agree.

mandate: the wishes or support of the people as expressed by their vote.

mass media: sources of information, including radio, television, newspapers, and magazines, that influence a large number of people.

mass transit: a system of moving people from place to place by public conveyance, such as train, bus, ferry, or subway.

mayor-council: a form of municipal government in which the voters elect both a mayor and a council to govern.

Medicaid: joint federal-state program to aid the poor in paying for medical expenses.

Medicare: federal social insurance program for those over 65.

merger: combing of two or more entities, as in court merger—the combining of trial courts.

merit employment: the practice of hiring and promoting employees on the basis of objective, unbiased, competitive testing.

message of necessity: a message from the governor to the legislature requesting an immediate vote on a bill.

misdemeanor: a lesser crime, generally punishable by less than one year in prison.

moral obligation bonds: provision in an authority's enabling act that requires the state to restore any deficiencies in the fund supporting the bonds.

municipality: a political unit, such as a town, city, or village, incorporated for local self-government.

nominating convention: the meeting of party delegates in a gubernatorial or presidential election year to nominate candidates and to write a platform.

nomination: the process of proposing or naming a candidate for elective office.

nonrenewable: a natural resource that is depleted with use.

nuclear power: the power produced from the energy released by an atomic reaction.

original jurisdiction: the authority of a court to hear and to decide a case for the first time.

override: the power of a legislature to pass a law after the executive (governor) has vetoed it.

pardon: an executive order that frees a person from punishment or legal consequences of a crime.

petit jury: also called **trial jury.** A group of impartial people who evaluate evidence and determine an accused person's guilt or innocence.

petition: a formal request signed by a number of citizens and addressed to a government or other authority.

pigeonhole: to kill a bill by refusing to take action on it or pass it out of committee.

platform: a political party's declaration of principles and policies.

plea bargaining: a practice in which a criminal defendant is, under certain conditions, allowed to plead guilty to a lesser charge without a trial, usually resulting in a lenient sentence.

plurality: highest number of votes.

political action committee (PAC): a legal entity set up by a special-interest group to collect and spend funds for a political purpose.

political party: an organization of citizens who work together to elect candidates and to set public policy.

politics: participation in political affairs.

pre-file: to file a bill before the regular legislative session begins.

presidential primary: a party election in which voters choose the candidate they want their convention delegates to nominate.

primary: an election to determine the nominees of a political party. In New York State, a voter must be enrolled in a political party to vote in the party's primary.

private law: *see* **civil law**.

probable cause: reasonable grounds for believing that a crime has been committed and that the person arrested is the one who committed it.

property tax: a tax imposed on real or personal property.

prosecuting attorney: the government's legal representative who brings charges and attempts to prove a crime has been committed.

public assistance: aid programs funded by federal and state dollars available to those who can prove they are in need.

public defender: an attorney employed by the state and appointed by the court to defend persons unable to afford legal assistance.

public domain: owned by the public; not subject to copyright law.

public law: part of the legal system that deals with the relationship between government and its citizens.

public utility: a company supplying gas, electricity, or water to the public under the oversight of an agency of the government.

quorum: a minimum number of members of a group required to conduct business.

quota: a required or assigned percentage.

ratification: a process for formally approving a law, treaty, or constitution.

real property: land, including the buildings or improvements on it, and its natural assets.

reapportionment: the redistribution of representation in a legislative body according to changes in the census figures.

recess: a brief period during which the legislature is not in session.

recession: a mild, short-term economic slump.

redistrict: to redraw the boundaries of legislative districts.

referendum: the submission of a proposed law to the vote of the electorate.

registration: the act of formally entering one's name on the election rolls by swearing that one is a citizen, 18 years of age or older, and a resident of the election district for the requisite amount of time.

regulation: a rule by a government agency or department for the purposes of enforcing a law

regulatory agency: an administrative part of government that carries out laws.

renewable: a resource that can be replaced, such as timber.

representative: a person who represents a constituency in a legislative body; a member of Congress.

representative democracy: a form of government in which a small group of people is elected to act for or on behalf of a constituency in exercising a voice in legislation.

reserved powers: powers of the states. Those powers that the U.S. Constitution neither gives to the national government nor denies to the states.

residency: a requirement that voters must live in an election area for a certain amount of time before they are eligible to vote there.

revenue: income of a government from all sources appropriated for the payment of public expenses.

revenue sharing: a form of government financing by which a portion of money collected in federal income tax is returned to the state and local government.

right-to-work law: a state law that allows a person to obtain and to keep a job without joining a labor union.

save harmless: a provision of the financing of public school law that states that a district will not receive less state aid than it did in the previous year.

school board: locally elected or appointed body that governs a school district.

school district: an area within a state defined by state government to administer the public schools of that area.

senate: a body of lawmakers in government. The "upper house" of the New York State Legislature.

sentence: punishment decided by a court.

separation of powers: division of the legislative, executive, and judicial functions of government into three branches.

sheriff: the chief representative of the courts in certain counties.

small claims court: a minor court that hears civil cases involving small amounts of money, usually no more than $2,000.

social welfare: organized public and private social services for the assistance of disadvantaged classes or groups.

solid waste: garbage and trash.

special district: a unit of local government set up to provide services that a local government does not provide, such as fire protection and water supply.

special session: legislative session called by the governor and limited to subjects put forth by the governor.

"spoils system": *see* **civil service.**

sponsor: a member of the legislature who introduces a bill.

state: an independent political unit characterized by population, territory, government, and sovereignty.

state of the state: the constitutionally required annual report of the Governor of New York State to the legislature, outlining the government's past accomplishments and future goals.

subpoena: a court order requiring a person to appear as a witness.

sunset laws: laws that require certain state agencies and programs to be reviewed regularly by the state legislature; an agency or program is automatically abolished if it cannot be proven essential.

sunshine law: a law requiring government agencies to hold open meetings and to give advance notice of these meetings.

superfund: congressional appropriations, beginning in 1980, to be used by the EPA for nationwide hazardous waste cleanup.

table: a parliamentary motion to "kill" a bill.

tax base: the total assessed value of all property in a community.

three-day rule: requires that bills awaiting passage by either house must sit three legislative days before a final vote may be taken.

toxic waste: the hazardous and often poisonous byproducts of chemical manufacturing.

trial jury: *see* **petit jury.**

true bill: a grand jury's agreement with a prosecutor that the evidence warrants a trial.

two-party system: a political system in which two major groups with differing political philosophies compete for control of the government.

unalienable right: *see* **inalienable right.**

unconstitutional: pertaining to a law not allowed by the constitution.

unemployment compensation: a government payment under the Social Security Act to persons who lose their jobs through no fault of their own.

union: an association of people or states that join together for a common purpose.

urban renewal: the improving or rebuilding of declining downtown areas of cities.

user's fee: a revenue collected for consumption of a service, such as metered water or electricity.

venue: location of a trial.

veto: power of a chief executive to prevent a bill from becoming a law. A veto may be overridden by a vote of the legislature.

will: a legal document made by a person directing what should be done with his or her property after the person's death.

withholding: an automatic deduction from wages or salary used to prepay income tax.

workers' compensation: payments required by law to be made to an employee who is injured or becomes ill on the job.

write-in candidate: a candidate whose name does not appear on the ballot and whose name must be written on the ballot by supporters.

zoning: regulations for use or occupancy of land.

SELECTED BIBLIOGRAPHY

Access to Health Care. New York: League of Women Voters of New York State, 1992.

Action in Albany. Current legislative priorities. New York: League of Women Voters of New York State, 1994.

Annual Report, New York State Commission on Judicial Conduct. New York: Commission on Judicial Conduct, 1994. (Annual from 1985)

"Canon 7 of the Code of Judicial Conduct," *Tenth Annual Report, New York State Commission on Judicial Conduct.* New York: Commission on Judicial Conduct, 1985. Adopted by the New York State Bar Association and the American Bar Association.

A Citizen's Guide to the APA (Adirondack Park Agency) Land Use Regulations. Albany: APA, State of New York, 1980. (Pamphlet)

The Citizen Lobbyist. Techniques for lobbying in Albany. New York: League of Women Voters of New York State, 1993.

The Courts of New York—A Guide to Court Procedures, with a Glossary of Legal Terms. New York: Committee on Courts and the Community of the New York State Bar Association, 1993. (Pamphlet)

Directory of New York State Officers & Officials. Includes photos and committee assignments, meeting times, state agencies, and more. New York: League of Women Voters of New York State, 1994-95. (Annual)

Domestic Violence. New York: League of Women Voters of New York State, 1994.

The Elusive Quest: The Struggle for Equality of Educational Opportunity. By Edwin Margolis & Stanley Moses (Foreword by Governor Mario M. Cuomo). New York: The Apex Press, 1992.

Environmental Quality Bond Act 1986—Annual Report 1987. Albany: New York State Department of Environmental Conservation and New York State Office of Parks, Recreation, and Historic Preservation, 1987.

Factbook—April 1991. Albany: New York State Department of Environmental Conservation, 1991.

Facts for Voters. New York: League of Women Voters of New York State, 1994. (Pamphlet)

Government and Politics in New York: A Selected Guide to Information Sources. Comp. by Robert B. Harmon. (Public Information Series.) Monticello, IL: Vance Bibliographies, 1990.

The Judicial Maze. Complete guide to New York's court system. New York: League of Women Voters of New York State, 1990.

Low Level Radioactive Waste. New York: League of Women Voters of New York State, 1990.

Merit Selection of Judges: Questions and Answers. New York: League of Women Voters of New York State, 1994.

New York State Department of Transportation Annual Report. Albany: New York State Department of Transportation, 1992. (Annual from 1987)

The New York State Directory, 1994-95. 12th edition. Provides direct information access to officials in the three branches of government; lists key contacts in public information offices and libraries; classifies government activity into 25 major policy areas; and more. San Mateo, CA: Walker Western Research, 1994.

New York State in the Year 2000. Ed. by Jeryl L. Mumpower and Warren F. Ilchman. Albany: State University of New York Press, 1988.

New York State Today: Politics, Government, Public Policy. Ed. by Jeffrey Stonecash, John K. White, and Peter W. Colby. 3rd edition. Albany: State University of New York Press, 1994.

Road to the Voting Booth (Part 3). Conducting a successful registration drive. New York: League of Women Voters of New York State, 1994.

"Rules Governing Judicial Conduct," *Tenth Annual Report, New York State Commission on Judicial Conduct.* Promulgated by the Chief Administrative Judge of the Unified Court System of the State of New York. New York: Commission on Judicial Conduct, March 1985.

State of New York 1994 Election Law. Albany: New York State Board of Elections, 1994.

Treatise on New York Environmental Law. By Nicholas Robinson. New York: New York State Bar Association, 1992.

Understanding the NYS Legislature. Pocket guide. New York: League of Women Voters of New York State, 1994.

Women and the Law. Covers the financial and equality issues of women. New York: League of Women Voters of New York State, 1994.

INDEX